Rebecca has written the anthem for a slow and rich life that we all need to hear! Refreshing and poignant, *A Better Life* illuminates a different path forward for us—one of intentionality and reliance on God's leading. Thank you, Rebecca, for championing little by little steps forward and helping us see how they add up in such beautiful ways. A must-read!

LARA CASEY, CEO of Cultivate What Matters,
author of *Cultivate* and *Make It Happen*

Rebecca is the kind of friend you want to have coffee with every day. She's a soft place to land—full of empathy. But her words always stir me to more—she speaks truth. This book is like the world's best coffee date: a story full of redemption and mission and the grace of God but also a call to slow down so we can follow him more clearly to what he's prepared for us.

JESS CONNOLLY, author of *You Are the
Girl for the Job* and *Take It Too Far*

There is a magic in slowing down that Rebecca illustrates so beautifully in *A Better Life*. This is the permission slip you need to lean in—lean in to small signs and quiet beginnings, to moments when you feel a tug at your heart, to hard times, and to failure. You'll catch yourself in a new pace in life after reading this book, and you'll never look back.

JESSICA HONEGGER, founder of Noonday
Collection, author of *Imperfect Courage*

A Better Life is not about stopping your ambition but channeling your ambition for something much bigger than you. God is in every detail of your calling, not just the end result. Inside these pages, Rebecca will show you how to slow down, trust God for every step, and see him do more than you could ever aspire to do on your own.

MICHELLE MYERS, founder of she works HIS way

Rebecca lives the kind of life that's rich in hope and vision and step-by-step obedience. I've had a front-row seat, and I'm glad to have her words now to encourage and inspire us all to live our own better life.

HAYLEY MORGAN, author of *Preach to Yourself*, coauthor of *Wild and Free*

If you've ever worried that your life is too ordinary to make a difference in the world or that a passion for social justice requires a passport and a plane ticket, then this is the book for you. Rebecca invites us into her Detroit neighborhood and shows us that all you really need is to open your front door and meet your neighbors. It's not always comfortable or convenient, but it is completely ordinary and totally game changing. Trust me, you'll look at your life and the people in it differently after this.

LISA-JO BAKER, bestselling author, cohost of the *Out of the Ordinary* podcast

This book is for the person who needs the comforting reassurance that they don't have to have it all figured out to make a difference. Rebecca has such a gift for being fully honest, transparent, and relatable. This message resonates with anyone who has a desire in their soul to change the world by starting small.

MOLLY STILLMAN, writer, stillbeingmolly.com, host of the *Business with Purpose* podcast

Rebecca spots God in the details of her life and makes readers excited to do the same for themselves. I loved every chapter more than the one before. This book ended too soon!

EMILY THOMAS, host of the *Mom Struggling Well* podcast

Rebecca drew me in from page one with her engaging storytelling, and I gained a newfound desire to have her as my next-door neighbor. But it was seeing Scripture come alive through her eyes that made this book a page-turner for me. As her powerful story unfolded, it reminded me once again that simple steps of obedience to a kingdom purpose truly do walk us toward not just a better life but the best life.

JEN SCHMIDT, author of *Just Open the Door*,
host of the Becoming Conference, blogger
at *Balancing Beauty and Bedlam*

Have you ever wanted to know what it would look like if you said yes to God—repeatedly? That is what Rebecca shares in *A Better Life*. Her life of obedience is both the inspiration and the challenge for readers to follow God, no matter where he leads or what he asks.

MALINDA FULLER, author of *Obedience Over Hustle*

a better life

a better life

Slowing Down to Get Ahead

REBECCA SMITH

ZONDERVAN BOOKS

A Better Life
Copyright © 2020 by Rebecca Smith

Requests for information should be addressed to:
Zondervan, *3900 Sparks Dr. SE, Grand Rapids, Michigan 49546*

Zondervan titles may be purchased in bulk for educational, business, fundraising, or sales promotional use. For information, please email SpecialMarkets@Zondervan.com.

ISBN 978-0-310-35759-9 (audio)

Library of Congress Cataloging-in-Publication Data

Names: Smith, Rebecca, 1983- author.
Title: A better life : slowing down to get ahead / Rebecca Smith.
Description: Grand Rapids : Zondervan, 2020. | Summary: "In her down-to-earth
    and helpful debut book, A Better Life: Slowing Down to Get Ahead, Rebecca
    Smith — the founder of Better Life Bags — shares her story of how God can use
    even the smallest decisions in our lives to lead us into big adventures as we love
    others right where we are"— Provided by publisher.
Identifiers: LCCN 2019034874 (print) | LCCN 2019034875 (ebook) | ISBN
    9780310357575 (trade paperback) | ISBN 9780310357582 (ebook)
Subjects: LCSH: Christian women—Religious life. | Christian life.
Classification: LCC BV4527 .S63355 2020 (print) | LCC BV4527 (ebook) | DDC
    248.4—dc23
LC record available at https://lccn.loc.gov/2019034874
LC ebook record available at https://lccn.loc.gov/2019034875

The author is represented by the literary agency of Alive Literary Agency, www
.aliveliterary.com.

Cover design: Connie Gabbert | Design + Illustration
Black fabric on cover: Better Life Bags
Blue fabric on cover: Emilie Fosnocht / patternbank
Interior design: Denise Froehlich

Printed in the United States of America

20 21 22 23 24 /LSC/ 10 9 8 7 6 5 4 3 2 1

For Neil. I'm so grateful to get to walk these days with you by my side. You are my best friend.

———————

To my precious kids, who remind me every day that this life is big and beautiful and funny and worth living.

———————

To my parents, who started this little life of mine back in 1983. Thank you for always being my biggest cheerleaders.

———————

And to the city of Hamtramck (Ham-tram-ick). You have captured my heart and will forever be my home.

Contents

Foreword

I recently sat in a circle with a handful of leaders from my community, trying to answer the question, "How might we make this place better?" The discussion centered on my neighborhood, a place creaking beneath the weight of poverty and vibrant by nature. Though each member of the circle does important work in this place I love, I was the only participant who lives in the neighborhood.

To my great relief, they listened. They heard my perspective. They jotted notes when I said, "Ask my neighbors what they need and what they offer." I did my best to speak without my voice cracking, vulnerably protective of this overlooked place that continues to teach me how to love, how to really *see*. Yes, it is complicated. It's also resilient. Hospitable. It's a shoes-off sort of place, messy and comfy. It comes bearing gifts.

Rebecca's home place reminds me so much of my own.

For months after moving into the neighborhood, I camped out in the story of Jesus feeding the four thousand (Mark 8). The crowd was growing restless. The disciples were wringing their hands in sheer panic. "Do something, Jesus!"

So he *did*.

Attentive to the energy level that was accelerating toward

"chaos," he looked his beloveds in the eye and asked one small question. "How much bread do you have?"

God, vibrantly alive on every city street and country road, invites us to grab what we've got and join in the work of repair. This plan seems faulty at best. *"How much bread do you have?"* The longer I live with my life pressed up against lack, the more I understand the brilliant abundance of this question.

The book you're about to read is a journey of discovery, a trek away from self and toward discomfort. You will watch as growth unfolds, hardship tangled up with triumph. Rebecca is forthright about her early jitters, open-handed with her mistakes, and above all, enthusiastic about the ripple effects of mutual generosity. Her "bread" was a cowhide and some courage. Her neighbors buttered it with grit, skill, and trust. Voilà! A feast of hope and sisterhood, with the capacity to transform each woman's life, especially Rebecca's.

What does it really take to make life better? I hope my community continues to circle up around this question while remaining mindful of the power of everyday presence. Living with our bodies low to the ground grants us the perspective necessary for joining the hard work of collective flourishing.

The prophet Jeremiah instructs us that the welfare of our neighbors determines our own welfare (Jeremiah 29:7). Obedience is small and slow. It is the daily showing up and the stubborn sticking around. It is listening. Yielding. Capturing an imaginative vision for seeing beauty where many do not.

Growth happens in the details—"life as a daily protest," Rebecca writes. Lean in as she shares what it looks like to settle in, tear down fences, and share our daily bread.

Shannan Martin, author of *The Ministry of Ordinary Places* and *Falling Free*

Introduction

Special Stickers

||||||||||||||||||||||||||||||||||||||||||||||||||||||||||||||||||||||||

I suppose when I think about it, this story starts with a sticker—a bright, round, orange sticker that spelled S-P-E-C-I-A-L in black letters. I found this sticker one day in college on my way home from class. Stuck to the pavement, it had been ignored and trampled by hundreds of feet, but I saw it and leaned over to pick it up. It was a gift. And I knew exactly whom it was from. Here was a message telling me I was special and seen and loved and known and thought of.

Now, after you learn that I lived right next to a grocery store, you might try to convince me that finding this sticker was no big deal. You might point out that stickers such as this are used to mark and differentiate among various types of deli sandwiches. You might try to explain that this sticker was simply a note to let customers know that the sandwich inside contained avocado or mayo or a pickle and somehow had ended up outside—probably discarded by a hungry undergrad eating lunch while running off to take a final exam.

But you would be wrong.

It was a love letter to me from God. I stuck that sticker on the back of my college ID, and it reminded me of God's secret message to me every time I pulled it out.

I was seen by him. He wasn't far away, orchestrating the events of my life from a high pedestal or behind a closed curtain. He was near, close enough to plant this little round sticker in a place where he knew I would see it and pick it up.

God knew exactly where I would be walking that day. My path was not a surprise to him. He knew exactly where I had come from and where I was going next, because he had planned it. It was his joy to leave little gifts for me, his daughter, as I journeyed along this path.

I couldn't believe this was the first time I had noticed one. Had they been there all along and I had just never slowed down to see them? Over the next several years, I became better at recognizing the messages from God when I saw or heard them. And it would become my joy to find them. A game of hide-and-seek. An ongoing Easter egg hunt. My eyes remained open to noticing the whispers and the messages and the special "stickers" God sent my way. And I learned to go slow enough to have time to bend down and scrape the message off the cement.

Like a daughter desperate to hear the voice of her father, I started looking for these gifts more and more. And I found them. They came in the form of a Bible verse that spoke directly to the heartbreak I was experiencing, followed by a sermon at church that shared on the same verse. They came on the back of a moving vehicle—a personalized license plate or bumper sticker that spelled out a message of hope and promise right when my heart was swirling with questions and doubt. And they came in the form of two solid wood dressers— dumped by someone in the alley behind my house on the very day that I was lamenting my collection of cheap furniture that was falling apart.

These are the moments many would see as coincidences. But I knew they weren't. I knew that God wanted to send me a gift and orchestrated the timing and the message and the perfect way they all came together. They resembled little bread-crumbs dropped along my path, signs from my Father that I was on the right—or wrong—path. I didn't know where my path was leading, but these strategically placed breadcrumbs—these special stickers—reminded me that Someone did know. Someone had a destination and a plan for my life, and I simply needed to follow the stickers.

Each chapter in this book highlights a sticker I've found along my way or the lesson that a sticker led me to. They are reminders that my path has been paved by a God who cares about the big dreams and the small moments. It can be tempting to think I'm paving my own path in this life. That's the message preached on motivational Instagram accounts, after all. They say my destination and my goals are up to me to achieve by my own effort. But the truth is that God has gone before me with a street paver to clear the way, and while the cement is drying and I'm figuring out my next step, he plants reminders that he's there. That he is close. That he has a plan and that his plan is good. That he sees me and my dreams and wants to help me achieve them in a way that is life-giving and manageable and full of peace.

I know I'm not alone in this. He drops special stickers for you too. Think about that moment when you ruined dinner and a friend showed up on your porch with a hot, steamy roasted chicken just an hour later. That is a gift. Or on the anniversary of a miscarriage, when rainbows showed up everywhere—embroidered on the front of your toddler's shirt, references in the songs played on the radio, and the day ending with an actual double rainbow when the weather predicted no rain. Those are gifts. Or the time when finances were really tight and rent was due in two days. You didn't know where the money would come from, but suddenly a check for the exact amount appeared in your mailbox in an unmarked envelope. What an unexpected, undeserved, unbelievable gift.

These gifts are waiting for us along our path to a better life. We don't have to do anything to receive them except slow down and notice. Most of the time, we can only see these gifts when we walk slowly and observantly, eyes on our own feet and not the journey of another. Our gifts are personalized and can be noticed only by the one receiving them.

Maybe your gifts are bigger than mine, or a different shape and color—less deli-sandwich-sticker-like. But they are there, waiting for you to find them. Each one can add something unique to your life. Some may be small messages of hope, and others may be large miraculous moments. But they turn an ordinary life into something extraordinary. You will stand back and look at your life in ten or twenty or thirty years with amazement—realizing that somehow this routine of waking up every day and falling asleep at night, the days filled with moments of desperation and times of joy, has transformed into a better life than anything you could have dreamed of.

I'm not sure where you are in your journey. Maybe you heard that if you hustled hard enough, you would make it to the top. So you tried, but you're so tired. Maybe someone told you that God is not in a hurry. But you are, and you're anxious to make more money and gain more success. Maybe someone told you that you are in charge of your future. But you've been steering your life the way you want it to go, and it's not working. Maybe you need to hear there is a better way. When you give up the try-hard feelings and the striving toward a finish line that seems to keep moving, you have time to feel the soft breeze and enjoy the journey. When you stay even when it is hard, you grow deep roots of stability. And when you go slow enough to notice the gifts, you end up way ahead.

CHAPTER 1

Stand Down

When You Beg God to Fix It
and He Tells You to *Be Still*

||||||||||||||||||||||||||||||||||||||||||||||||||||||||||||||||||||||||

O f all the sounds and smells of my childhood, the most memorable is the sound of dial-up internet. I recently found a clip of this soundtrack to my youth and played it for my nine-year-old son, Jonah. We listened to twenty-eight seconds of squealing, beeping, dinging, and static as I explained to him that at the end of this nonsense, we would finally be connected to the invisible realms of internet land. His eyes were wide with disbelief.

"You mean . . . we still aren't connected to the internet?" he exclaimed as the sound effects seemed to go on endlessly.

"Nope," I replied. "And in fact, when we did finally connect to the internet, our phone line would be tied up." Since he grew up without a landline, this made even less sense to him. So I had to explain that once upon a time, our phones were plugged permanently into the wall and that everyone in the family shared the same phone number. And if our computer was connected to the internet, no one could call us on the phone—even in an emergency. Being on the internet made you feel rushed and anxious because you always wondered whose call you were missing while you were browsing the World Wide Web. His little mind couldn't process the idea that we haven't always been hyperconnected to one another via FaceTime, text messaging, or email. Even I can hardly believe how much technology has changed in just twenty years.

Somewhere between 2001 and 2005—the years I spent as an undergrad—dial-up internet faded away, and suddenly we could talk on the phone and be on the internet at the same time. It transitioned so seamlessly that I'm not sure any of us recognized the change until it had already happened. Most of us had our own cell phones at this point—complete with free nights and weekends.

I spent the last two years of college exploring the boundaries of the internet, specifically online journals (the word *blog* had not yet been invented) such as Xanga and LiveJournal. I poured my young, tender heart out on those virtual pages. I typed away tirelessly, sitting in the back bedroom of apartment #412 that I shared with three other girls. We each had our own bedroom, graduating from the cramped quarters of freshman and sophomore dorms into the luxury apartments reserved for upperclassmen. And for the first time in our lives, each of us had our own computer and, along with that, access to the world in a way we'd never imagined.

In 2005 Facebook was an elite community reserved for students from select colleges. You needed a collegiate email address ending in .edu to join, and they opened access to this new social platform to only a few colleges at a time. Months before we graduated, Facebook allowed students from our school to create a Facebook profile, and we all signed up—thus expanding our connectivity from AOL Instant Messenger and chat rooms to being able to follow along with everyone's daily updates on their Facebook profile walls. We could now see where everyone was on a Friday night, how our best friend felt about her term paper grade, and where our college crush was moving after graduation.

|||||||||||||||||||||||||||||||||||||||||||||||||||||||||||||||||||||||||||||||||

I confess to being an internet girl through and through. I joined early—jumped in with both feet—and still love the connectedness and opportunity being online allows us today. When I have a gaggle of children clinging to my shins, I can pull out my phone and catch up with actual adult friends and have adult texting conversations without packing everyone up for a playdate. I've seen friends take webinars and online classes from the comfort of their living rooms to further a career or start a new one. Groceries ordered online and delivered right to my doorstep? Yes, please. And I found out the other day that I can even get evaluated by an online doctor without having to set foot in a germ-infested waiting room or bring all four of my kids along with me.

Sure, there are days when all this access and connectivity drives me crazy and makes me compare my life with those I see on the tiny Instagram squares on my phone. I see Crystal repainting her house, and my eyes drift up from my phone to land on the fingerprints and on the chips of paint coming off my own living room walls. I suddenly feel the need to repaint too. I watch Melody share about the homeschooling curriculum she's gathering and planning for the fall, and I second-guess our family's decision to send our kids to a new charter school down the road after years of homeschooling.

Emily pulls out homemade chocolate chip cookies from the oven to celebrate the last day of school, and I look at a pantry that needs to be restocked and feel sorry that my kids don't have a better mom who knows how to cook and bake.

When I finally put my phone down, I realize that sometimes I long for more simple and quiet days. The days when I didn't know what everyone got for Christmas or Mother's Day unless I went over to their houses to see. Or the times when we couldn't just pull out our phones at the dinner table to google the answer to everyone's curiosity about who played the voice of Aladdin in the original movie. Sometimes I long for the simpler days when we weren't so easily accessed by phone, text, or email and then expected to reply instantly.

Sure, the internet has its downsides. But mostly I love it. I've always loved it. The internet has carried me to places I never could have gone on my own—and served as the platform that allowed me to grow a custom handbag company, Better Life Bags, from a small Etsy shop to a million-dollar business with employees, a local storefront, and, of course, a website. I don't know where I would be today without the invention of the internet. Like the key to a secret garden, it has opened doors and dreams and pathways that would never have been previously accessible.

|||||||||||||||||||||||||||||||||||||||||||||||||||||||||||||||||||||||||||||||||||

The internet had not only allowed us this new way to connect and follow the daily adventures of our friends and classmates beyond graduation, it allowed us to meet new people that we otherwise would never cross paths with. Not long after I joined Facebook, my eye caught the next shiny, new internet-y thing— online dating. I had somehow gotten through four years of college without finding my husband. I'll admit, I had gone to college to get an education, yes—but also to find a husband. Call me old-fashioned, but getting married and starting a family had been a dream of mine since I was four years old.

I wanted to be a mom more than anything in life, and I felt that college was just four years standing in my way of achieving that dream. But to please society and my parents, I chose a major and attended four years of college. Really, I was only going to class to find a husband. If I could have majored in housekeeping or mothering, I probably would have.

To me, every boy I sat next to in class had the potential to be the Mr. to my Mrs., but while I tried on a lot of last names during those four years, none of them panned out. I found myself single at graduation. There was no Mrs. degree attached to my name. This hadn't been part of my plan, but it was where I found myself.

And the degree I finally settled on because it was as close to a "parenting" degree as I could get—elementary education— was also going to have to sit on the shelf for a bit. Right before graduating, I invited my parents over to my apartment for a home-cooked meal to inform them that while I was grateful they had paid for all four years of a private university, I was going to file my degree away for the time being and head off to California to be a missionary in the inner city of Bakersfield—a position I became aware of through my local campus ministry.

I was going to work with troubled youth in the poorest county in California. I needed an adventure to go on since planning a wedding wasn't a part of my postgraduate life, and I felt as though maybe my life would find purpose there.

I spent the summer after graduating from college raising financial support for this one-year adventure on the other side of the country. In between meeting with people and asking them for money, I signed up for a ten-day free trial of an online dating website called ChristianCafe.com.

As I filled in the personal information that would be sure to cast me in the best light, I thought, *I'll probably meet someone on here, and for the rest of my life, I'll have to tell everyone that we met on the internet.* How shameful. How embarrassing. How completely desperate. Online dating back then was nothing like it is today. We didn't swipe left (or is it right?) until we found someone who looked attractive and interesting. It was sort of a last-resort method reserved for the hopeless and aging, not ideal for a freshly graduated twenty-something with a college degree and her whole life ahead of her. But I was bored and curious and hoped to get my marriage plans back on track, so I pushed through those feelings.

Sure enough, I stumbled upon Neil's profile in those first ten days. He mentioned in it that someday he wanted to live in the less-than-desirable areas of the world, which intrigued me because of the adventure I was about to embark on. He also was a soldier in the army, currently deployed to Iraq. My heart skipped a beat thinking about this man in uniform. In a war zone no less. Really, it was probably my American duty to contact him. He was my knight in shining armor, defending the nation so I could live free.

I waited for what seemed like days, but was really only hours, for his response to my initial contact request, logging in multiple times to see if he had responded. He tells me now that it was love at first profile sight for him. He wrote back and started our daily communication, asking each other every question we could think of to get to know each other over the virtual connection of email. We then moved to Instant Messenger, where our questions and answers became even more instantaneous.

I would leave my computer speakers on full volume at night because with the time difference between the United States and Iraq, Neil was often only available to chat after my bedtime. When that iconic creaky door sound emerged from the speakers, signaling that someone had just signed on to AOL Instant Messenger, I would immediately jump out of bed. It was always Neil, ready to chat into the early hours of the morning.

In October he decided to call me. After we had talked incessantly with our fingers for two months, I heard Neil's actual voice. I had moved to California at this point, and during the middle of the day, while I was figuring out the next few weeks of lesson plans for the after-school kid's club I ran at a local church in Bakersfield, my phone rang. The long string of unfamiliar numbers on my cell phone screen—signaling a long-distance call—made my heart stop. I knew who this was.

"Hello?" I was trembling. "Hey," he said. And I was gone. He had me at hello. Drop the mic. End the call—no, don't do that. Let's talk forever. I was smitten with that voice.

We talked every day for months. I would lie on my bed whispering into the phone after all my new California roommates had fallen asleep. My words traveled all the way to Iraq, where Neil sat on a hard metal chair after waiting in line to use the internet phones. Our thirty-minute time allotment would go so fast that he would hang up, give the phone to another soldier wanting to call home for his thirty minutes, and wait in line again to start the routine over until I couldn't keep my eyes open any longer.

In December he flew home to Georgia, where he was stationed. His deployment was over, and he asked if he could come to California to visit me in person. We had talked about everything under the sun—the Bible, our dreams, our pasts, our hobbies, and our fears. It only made sense that meeting in person would be the next step.

Neil called my dad to ask for his permission to fly out to meet me, and my dad asked Neil for actual references he could call. References. To date his daughter. With phone numbers he actually called to find out more about this Neil guy. I was so embarrassed. But also relieved to know that the person I'd been chatting with and falling in love with over the last few months was exactly who he had said he was—and not a serial killer.

On the drive down I-5 to the LA airport to pick up my soldier, I followed a car with this license plate: Smithx2. Smith was Neil's last name. Could I be his x2? Could this be a sign that we were for sure going to get married? Was this a special sticker telling me I was on the right path? Wedding bells started ringing in my ears, but I told myself I couldn't be sure. I did, however, snap a grainy picture of the plate on my flip phone—just in case. Then I promised myself I would never do online dating again if this didn't work out.

When he stepped off that plane and wrapped his arms around me, the whole world stopped, shifted, and fell perfectly back into place—but this time with Neil by my side. Everything was working out perfectly. I was definitely his Smith x2. It was as if we had known each other all our lives.

Our relationship progressed quickly—as many things do in the internet age.

Almost exactly one year after joining Facebook and having my world expanded exponentially under my fingertips, Neil and I picked out an engagement ring—on an internet website, of course. It seemed as though anything and everything could be done online now. It was as if we had never lived without it. We probably could have even found a website that would legally marry us, but some things are best left to offline tradition.

We weren't engaged yet, but we were well on our way. And the ring I'd picked out was on its way to Georgia, as was I in a few months, with my first contracted teaching position starting that fall. Turns out I'd use my college degree after all, Mom and Dad.

| | | | | | | | | | | | | | | | | | | | | | | | | | | | | | | | | | | | | | | | | | | | | | | | | | | | | | | | | | | | | | | | | | | | |

Everything seemed to be going exactly as planned. Sure, I was a year or so behind my original marriage plans, but with any luck, I would be living my dream of wedding planning in just a few weeks. Neil would be on an airplane heading to California to join my family for vacation—with the ring. He was going to propose, and I was ready.

Until I got a call from him one day.

"I don't know if I'm supposed to be married," I heard him say over my flip phone as I walked laps around the block. This was my common practice to get in shape for the wedding. I had even gone to get my nails done at the salon the day before so they would be ready for the Facebook photos we would post later that week announcing our engagement. My nails were ready. Never mind my heart, which was about to get a wake-up call.

"Huh?" I responded. It came completely from left field. No, make that outer space. How could this man who had just bought my engagement ring not have already asked himself this question?

"I mean," he continued, "I'm not sure I ever asked God about our relationship and heard from him if this was the direction he wanted us to head. I think I need to assume that I should remain single unless God tells me otherwise."

I was mad. Hurt. Floored. Upset. Angry. Stunned. But my

only response was this: "Well, you need to figure that out without me. I'm not going to sit around and be dragged through the mud when you aren't sure if you are even supposed to be married."

Breaking up hadn't crossed his mind, so maybe he hung up as equally shocked as I was.

Smith x2 was now divided by 2. Everything had been going as planned. Marriage and starting a family had been within reach. This was the closest I'd ever gotten to making those dreams a reality, and it was all slipping through my fingers so fast. The tighter I tried to hold on, the faster it felt as if it were fading away.

Should I still move to Georgia? I had signed a contract with an elementary school in the town where Neil lived. Could I even break the contract? I had been invited to live with a family Neil knew personally who had promised to mentor me in my faith. Would they still want to?

And maybe the biggest question of all, the one Neil found himself asking: Had I ever asked God about our relationship? Or had I barged on ahead, assuming that such a good thing would have to have come from God? I mean, God had seen that license plate too, right? He wouldn't send a sticker like that just to tease me, would he? Would God dangle in front of me the thing I wanted more than anything and then take it away? Does he do that?

||||||| |||||| || |||||| ||||||||||||||||||||||| |||| ||||||||||| |||| |||||

Every time I looked at my left hand, it felt empty without that beautiful diamond ring we had picked out. I felt as if I had nothing left. God had stripped away the very thing I had been working so hard for. We were almost there. We had almost made it. And then it was all gone.

I set aside some of those hurt feelings and the anger I felt at God and lay down on the nappy carpet of my California apartment. I knew that when times got really tough, we should cry out to God. So I picked up my Bible off my bedside table and started reading. Daily.

The more I read the stories of people in the Bible going on big journeys and being asked to do really big things, the more I saw them move when God said move and wait when God said wait. But they weren't always good at knowing the difference, and sometimes they moved when God said wait and waited when God said move. But I could see that good things happened when they listened to God. And bad things happened when they didn't.

Maybe I needed to do this too—listen to what God's direction was for my life before charging ahead full speed or trying to change course to feel more comfortable. I wanted to call Neil back and tell him that I had made a mistake in breaking up, that we could remain together while he did some deep soul-searching about his future. I wanted to move, chase after Neil, and get that dream of being married back on the table.

Instead, I got really quiet and tried to listen for God's direction. When I read about God's promise to the currently barren Sarah and Abraham that they would have generations of children, I heard "wait." After reading about Daniel in the pit with the lions yet remaining untouched, I heard "stand down." I heard "keep your hands off" when God instructed his people not to touch the ark of the covenant as they carried it through the desert and into the land promised to them. When the ark started to wobble because the oxen carrying it stumbled, a man reached out to steady it—ultimately touching the ark—and he was struck down dead. I felt a parent's angst and heartbreak as a father ran after Jesus, upset that his daughter was dying, knowing that Jesus could save her. Instead of rushing to heal the girl, Jesus lingered a few more days, and I heard "I know it doesn't look like it, but I've got this in my control." It seemed obvious that God was telling me to keep my hands at my sides. I shouldn't touch the situation and try to make it work out in my favor. I should leave it alone and watch him move the pieces around the chessboard to make everything still work out in my favor. After all, everything he does is for our good.

These two commands—"stand down," coming from God, and "charge forward," coming from me—were at war with each other.

Have you been there too? The seas are raging, and your boat is rocking. This boat you built for yourself was supposed to take you to where you wanted to be—where your dreams lived. Dreams of getting married, being a mom, earning the degree, retiring early. But then a storm hits out of nowhere. He calls and breaks up with you. You struggle to get pregnant. You unexpectedly fail the last class you need to graduate. You lose your job two years before you'd planned to retire. You couldn't have seen any of it coming, but the clouds have rolled in, and the hail is hitting hard. This sudden storm in the middle of the journey was not in the plan, and now your boat is rocking out of control.

We don't like it, of course. No one likes being out in the open ocean in the middle of a storm. It's tempting to ask God why he would let us be on this boat in the first place. What kind of God would allow his child to experience such a storm?

We look for where Jesus is amid this storm and, just as the disciples did in Matthew 8:24, we see him sleeping. Sleeping! Can you believe it? How could he be sleeping? It's incomprehensible that anyone could sleep through the thunder and the waves and the rain. But he is. And since he is, it must mean that we need to fix everything ourselves because it doesn't look as if he's going to do anything about it. But here's what we miss when the waves are billowing up over the edge of the boat and drenching us as we hold on to the sides with all our might. This rocking boat in the middle of the storm is not out of control at all. It's completely within his control. Completely.

The infertility you are walking through is not unseen. God continues to hold you in the palms of his hands, using this experience to create a future and a family for you. The financial hardship you are facing isn't a surprise to God. He has not forgotten you and may be using this time to remind you that he does provide for all our needs. Your dreams of being married before you turned thirty were not wrong or embarrassing even as you round the corner to thirty-five. God is still working and orchestrating events in your favor. And the job you lost that seemed to mess up all future plans and paths that you worked so hard for? Maybe it's a redirection into something better and more suited for your life. He uses all things for good. Even this.

At this point in my own storm, I had to ask myself what I was going to do. Was I going to try to calm this storm on my own? Was I going to wake Jesus up with fits of screaming and terror? Was I going to reach out and try to steady the situation around me—even though God had already told me to keep my hands off it? Was I going to call on Jesus because I knew that with two words—be still—he could calm the storm raging around me as well as the storm in my heart?

I knew it was not my responsibility to convince Neil that we were to be married. It was not my job to orchestrate events and situations so that I would win in the end. At this point, the only directive I was hearing when I slowed down to listen was "keep your hands off." Every sermon I heard and every Bible story I read seemed to tell me to stand down, to wait it out.

The circumstances of my life were not how I wanted them. But I wasn't in charge of changing that. Neil had made a decision, and while I wanted to convince him of why he was wrong and how amazing it would be to be married, I knew I couldn't. I went about my life. I moved to Georgia, started my fifth-grade teaching position, and learned the ins and outs of the mind of a ten-year-old. I spent time in Bible studies and learning how to read my Bible and get something out of it. I made new friends and went to movies. Life went on while I waited for Neil's heart to change. Either his would change, or mine would. And it wasn't my place to change either of them. My only job was to follow God, to listen carefully to his whispers and his directions, and to do what they told me. I was in charge only of my obedience.

Sure, sometimes we need to step in and take action. But most of the time—especially for those of us with controlling tendencies—I think we will find that the best plan of action is to stand down. If your husband loses his job, don't hop right on Craigslist and apply for every position you find without even pausing. If your house seems dirty, don't neglect time spent playing board games with your kids to instead take a toothbrush to the baseboards. If your bank account seems low, don't rush off to take out a second mortgage on your house or sell your grandmother's diamonds. Just stand down for a second. Take a breath. And wait for direction.

In my own situation with Neil, thinking about all that scrambling to pick up the pieces of something that seemed to be falling apart left me with a sense of anxiety, unease, and exhaustion. And I was tired of that. I wanted to try God's way. I was going to wait and listen.

I wasn't going to make a dramatic effort to convince Neil to change his mind. And I wasn't going to jump right back into the dating scene in search of another potential husband who could help me get my wedding dreams back on track. I wasn't going to touch the crumbling mess falling down around me. I wasn't going to move. I would wait with my hands in the air and my feet firmly planted—a stance of surrender and worship.

I wasn't going to do anything except wait.

This practice of standing down and letting God walk before me was the first time in my life that I heard an almost audible command from him to keep my hands off. But it wouldn't be the last. It was the first in a long string of commands to step back and away from what he was trying to do. God had some big and exciting adventures planned that he knew I would love, and he didn't need me to get in the way of making them happen. "Stand down" became a life lesson I would carry with me for the next fifteen years. Even if my boat started rocking and Jesus seemed to be sleeping through the storm, I still was not supposed to touch anything—unless he told me to.

Despite taking a hands-off approach, I realized my dreams were not at stake. They were not at risk of being lost. Just the opposite. Dreams are best positioned for success when I listen to the directives of my Father and obey.

My obedience is what I'm in charge of, not anything else. God whispers, "This way," and I follow. He whispers, "Stay still," and I don't move. I've realized through this waltz of moving and swaying and standing that God was then—and is today—orchestrating a wonderful and beautiful and amazing path to my dreams and desires. Sometimes I had no idea where we were going, and I often ended up in places that never in my wildest dreams I thought I'd be. But in all of it, he is good. Following God rather than asking him to follow me might actually be the key to a life full of abundance and surprise and peace.

||||||||||||||||||||||||||||||||||||||||||||||||||||||||||||||||||||

Now that Neil and I lived in the same city, I saw him weekly. We were both involved in the same Bible study and friend group. I did my best not to manipulate situations or find out ahead of time if Neil would be attending an event before deciding whether or not I would go.

Each morning, I would get up before the sun, pop an everything bagel into the toaster, and sip coffee while I waited for the bagel to toast. When it popped out of the toaster, I would butter both sides and carry my breakfast into the dining room, where I'd sit down with my Bible, journal, buttery bagel, and coffee. While I ate, I learned how to read my Bible and hear God speak.

Perhaps I was more in tune to these stories and lessons from the Bible because of my specific situation, but after hearing the command to "stand down" and obeying, I started discovering a new directive. God was telling me that he could do the impossible. There is this incredible story in 1 Kings 18 that I read during this time in my life. Elijah was out to prove that his God was the true God. He had gathered quite the crowd and told the followers of Baal—a false god that many worshiped—to go collect an animal for an offering. They would both set out their offerings and ask their respective gods to send fire down to consume the offerings. Whichever offering was consumed by fire would show who the real God was and whose god was a fake. The followers of Baal laid their sacrifice out and yelled for their god to show up—for hours—to no avail.

Their god didn't send fire because their god wasn't real. When it was Elijah's turn, he prepared his offering to the true God and even drenched it with water—making it almost impossible to consume with fire. God did the impossible and sent down fire to lick up every last drop of water along with the sacrifice.

God was going to do the same for me—perform an impossible miracle. I just knew it.

I really wanted to be back together with Neil, but that seemed so impossible in light of his current pursuit of singleness. Yet I knew God could do the impossible. He could change Neil's heart, and I felt as though God was telling me that our story was not over, that I was still Neil's Smith x2. It was often hard to believe, and I was scared to say it out loud to anyone, but I held on to that promise and trusted that all these stories I was reading in my Bible were God speaking to me, promising to also do the impossible for me.

Months after the dream-killing phone call when Neil told me he didn't know whether he was supposed to get married to anyone—ever—I got another phone call from him. During that call, he explained that his period of seeking God was done and that he wanted us to be together again. I was thrilled and excited, and the butterflies in my stomach that had been caged up to protect my heart were let loose again. I could allow myself to experience feelings for Neil again—freely.

I had a feeling this dating period would be short. I knew he still had the ring. I'd seen it sitting on his dresser one day when I was over at his house for Bible study group. I'd walked down the hall to the bathroom and glanced in the open door to his room, and there it was, sitting on top of the dresser in plain sight. It took everything in me to stop myself from going in to look at it.

Thankfully, I didn't have to wait too long. That April, Neil and I met up with my family in Hilton Head, South Carolina, where they were vacationing. It was only a weekend trip since Neil and I were both working, but Hilton Head was within driving distance of Savannah, and we wanted to spend time with my family. In the back of my mind, I wondered whether this might be the weekend. But I'd been there before—gotten my hopes up about a trip where Neil would propose—and I'd been sorely let down. So I tried to not let my heart go there.

I still felt God impressing on me this idea of keeping my hands off everything in my life, including the timing of when Neil and I would get engaged and married. So I didn't ask Neil when he was planning on proposing. I didn't start looking through wedding magazines ahead of time. I didn't doodle my name with Smith at the end. I didn't name our children or plan our honeymoon, even though I wanted to. Instead, I remained content where I was—investing in friendships and digging into the Bible in a way I never had before. I dedicated myself to teaching and creating awesome lessons for my fifth-grade students. I lived my life, hoping that Neil would come around but not twiddling my thumbs until it happened.

While Neil and I browsed some gift shops on that trip, I remember coming across a cute picture frame with "Hilton Head" written on it. Verbally processing whether I should get it, I casually mentioned that I probably wouldn't end up buying it since this wasn't a large-scale or memorable trip. It was just a quick weekend getaway with my family.

When I heard Neil say under his breath, "It might be a big weekend," my heart jumped sixty feet in the air.

Had he brought the ring? I wondered as I carried the picture frame up to the cash register. Would there soon be a picture inside of two happy, in-love people with an engagement ring?

I'd soon find out.

The next morning, Neil woke me up early to go for a walk on the beach. We read our Bibles on a swinging bench overlooking the Atlantic Ocean as the sun peeked up, and then we went for a walk. We walked a long way. Even when I didn't think we could walk anymore, we kept on walking. He kept mentioning how surprised he was at how many people were out this early in the morning. And then, when he finally found a somewhat secluded spot with not as many people, he tripped.

He fell right on his face.

I laughed and reached out my hand to help him up. But he didn't get all the way up. He stayed down on one knee and asked me whether I would be his helper—his partner—in life forever. Cue the music and the flowers and the heart eyes emojis.

But I still hadn't heard those four magic words that I had waited so long to hear.

"Aren't you going to ask me?" I said as I stared down at him as he balanced on one knee and held the box open, with the ring sparkling brighter than the ocean water in the sun.

"I just did!" he exclaimed, seeming confused. "Will you marry me?"

I responded with a resounding yes. Of course I would! This time, we both knew it was right, and we were both ready. We had waited. We had sought God during that waiting. And he had led us both together. I hadn't manipulated or coerced events to line up this way. In fact, so much of our relationship had been out of my control, but all of it had been in God's control. And here I was again, finally seeing a dream come true, picking up another special sticker. This time my sticker—my gift from God—was in the form of a person. Every time I look at Neil, I'm reminded that he is a gift from God, one that was strategically placed along my path. When seasons in marriage get hard, I look back to these orchestrated moments that God used to bring us together and am reminded that this is good. This is right. God has given me a teammate I can journey through life with. And while we had no idea of the adventure we were about to embark on, I knew my first stop would be the local bookstore to buy some wedding magazines. I could finally start planning the wedding of my dreams!

CHAPTER 2

Bloom Where You're Planted

When You Try to Move to Iraq but End Up in Michigan

||||||||||||||||||||||||||||||||||||||||||||||||||||||||||||||||||||||

Perusing some Christian magazines one summer afternoon shortly after getting engaged, I came across the strangest advertisement. Some organization was looking for people who might be crazy enough to move to Iraq as missionaries. I couldn't show this to Neil fast enough. He had just been there. Iraq! Did he know that people—insane people, of course—moved there? On purpose?

Neil's time in Iraq with the military had been slowly and quietly changing his heart. He had experienced a different culture in ways I would never understand. He'd befriended translators and local coffee shop owners—some who ended up betraying their unit, pretending to be allies but passing on info and intelligence to the enemy, and others who ended up engaging in spiritual conversations about God and Jesus with Neil. One asked Neil whether he would be able to get him a Bible in Arabic. Neil was never able to do this before he left Iraq, and I think that still haunted him. So when he heard that maybe, possibly, he could go back, he wanted to. With all his heart.

There was only one problem. He would now have to take me with him—thanks to that ring on my left hand.

This whole engaged-to-be-married thing suddenly seemed a little more complicated than I'd realized. Would I move to Iraq if Neil wanted to go? What sort of future husband would even ask his more-precious-than-rubies wife to move to a war zone? Why had I even shown him that stupid ad? Should I even marry him? Thank goodness we were only engaged. I could easily get out of this crazy mess of a dream—which was looking more and more like a nightmare—if I wanted.

We were finally on our way to being married and starting a family together. I envisioned a quaint little home with a white picket fence and rocking chairs on the front porch. I didn't want to go to Iraq. Did Iraq even have white picket fences?

I felt the need to reach out and steady my once-again rocking boat. These new winds were starting to mess with the life I was trying to build. I wanted to stop Neil from taking me away from family. I wanted to prevent him from doing anything other than exactly what I wanted him to do. I needed to convince him that being a missionary in another country—especially Iraq—was a terrible idea.

Before freaking out, I decided to sit on my hands and ask God what he thought about this new idea of Neil's. Could I trust him with my future? My children? Our safety? Every time I read the Bible over the next few weeks and months, I simply underlined—in bright pink highlighter—wherever God talked about his love for the world. I'm sure you're not surprised to hear I used a lot of pink highlighter. God loves the world—all cultures, all nations—and he wants the world to love him too.

If Neil had a holy hankering to move to Iraq, maybe God had a grander purpose for us than a white picket fence. I could follow God even into a war-torn country, couldn't I? I hoped so.

So we got married in March 2008. And we prepared to move overseas.

One of those preparations was for Neil to take a vision trip to the country we ultimately settled on. Spoiler alert: it wasn't Iraq. After getting married, we joined up with a team of people our age who also wanted to move overseas for mission work. We combined Neil's desire and affinity for the Muslim people and culture with another team member's desire to live in East Asia. As it turns out, there is a small group of Muslim Chinese living in Western China. So while I was seven months pregnant with our first child, Jonah, Neil boarded a plane with two of our new teammates and headed for China.

This trip was hard—mostly for Neil. I was sitting comfortably in Savannah, Georgia. Well, as comfortable as you can be when you're seven months pregnant. Things in China weren't so easy for Neil. The language was confusing to him. The food stopped up his digestive system in the worst way possible. And a riot broke out between two cultural groups right outside Neil's hotel, resulting in the country shutting down the internet to censor everything. There was no longer any access to the outside world. There was no way for Neil to communicate with me and no way for me to reach him. I literally had no choice except to stand down and wait for the internet to start working again. It was terrifying, especially considering I was in the last trimester with our first baby.

What if something went wrong and I needed to reach him? What if the baby came early and I couldn't get ahold of him? After so many years of hyperconnectivity on the internet, to suddenly be without it felt isolating and alone.

After making it home—safely into my arms in the land of uncensored internet—Neil wisely decided that maybe before we moved all the way to a foreign country, we should gain some cross-cultural experience in America first. Maybe we should slow down and make a small move in the shallow side of the pool instead of a large jump into the deep end. Neither of us had lived anywhere where we were among the minority culture. Neither of us knew another language or even had many friends that didn't look like we did.

We googled "cities in America with a diverse and highly Muslim population." A few cities emerged in our results— Dearborn, Michigan, being one of them. We knew someone in Dearborn, someone we had met at a conference for cross-cultural ministry. After a brief phone call with a big ask—if we could move close to them for mentoring and training in cross-cultural ministry—we redirected our eyes from Western China to Southeast Michigan. Moving somewhere in America with a more diverse population than Savannah felt like the next right step. It was somewhere we could try something new with the safety net of our own country and familiarity to catch us if things went wrong. We would stay for two years and then make the leap across the world. We would be ready by then.

Six months after the birth of our first baby boy, we pulled off the interstate with all our belongings to settle in a city twenty minutes from Dearborn, Michigan, a city surrounded by Detroit called Hamtramck—the state's most diverse city. We definitely weren't in Savannah anymore. It was my first time seeing the city, and I wouldn't call it love at first sight.

Our friends drove us into town to our new rental house while I sat in the back seat wondering whether we could turn around and go back to Georgia. What was this place? It resembled a scene out of a movie—and not a romantic comedy or Hallmark movie. This place looked like a movie in which a zombie apocalypse had just taken place. Every other house seemed to be burned down, boarded up, or covered with graffiti. Signs on the street were printed in multiple languages, and instead of the weeping willow trees that hung over each side street in Savannah, Hamtramck had only street light poles. And only about 20 percent of them worked enough to light up the sidewalks at night. The Muslim call to prayer—a haunting melody sung over the loudspeakers of the local mosque—warred with the chiming of church bells down the street. Women covered from head to toe in black—a traditional Muslim abaya—pushed baby strollers filled with shopping bags on their way home from the Arab market. Polish flags waved proudly on homes of families who moved to this city in the 1940s to search for a better life. Markets advertised live chickens for sale, and record shops blaring the sound of Bob Marley catered to a newer population of young, vintage-loving millennials who were also moving into this eclectic melting pot of a city. Hanging on every street pole were signs that read "You fit in here." But did I? This was very different from anything and anywhere I had ever lived. But this was my new home. I lived here now.

We drove closer and closer to our rental house, turning left by a huge Catholic church and then right by the Polish meat market. Our friends explained that while Hamtramck is small—only two square miles—over twenty-six languages are spoken here. The city's slogan is "The World in Two Square Miles," which seemed accurate. I had thought we were moving somewhere familiar—somewhere in America—but this was far from anything I could have imagined. We were practically living in another country.

"Originally, the town was majority Polish until Bengali immigrants started pouring in during the eighties and nineties," our friends continued, trying to orient us to our new neighborhood. "Immigrants from Yemen, Bosnia, Afghanistan, Syria, and more have joined them since."

For people looking to move to a location with lots of diversity in order to dip their toes into what it might be like to move overseas, I think we landed in the right spot. But I wasn't sure I wanted to do this anymore.

Finally, we pulled up to our new home. I was hopeful as I stepped onto the cement porch. I enjoy making a home beautiful, and we were given a great deal on rent in exchange for painting and decorating the inside of the home. And it wasn't terrible. The kitchen had a quaint original 1950s ceramic sink that I loved bathing Jonah in. The back yard had raspberry bushes and a small patch of grass. I took to Pinterest and the local thrift store to shop for items that would make for a good home—baskets to hang on the wall, a glass cabinet door to turn into a dry-erase calendar, fresh paint, and slipcovers for the couches. This part was fun.

Then summer hit—and with it, the heat. The house we rented didn't have air conditioning. We would stuff our pillows in the freezer during the day so that at night we could have something with which to cool down in bed. Purchasing a window air conditioner didn't even cross our minds. We were here to "suffer for Jesus" and prepare for life overseas, and we assumed this meant no modern luxuries such as air conditioning. I would put Jonah to bed with only a diaper on, pointing the oscillating fan in his direction and hoping he wouldn't wake up in a pool of sweat.

Fourth of July came around mere weeks after moving into Hamtramck. Fireworks are legal in Michigan. All of them. Including the big dangerous ones that should be reserved for fireworks shows that happen over lakes with lots of space between the rockets and the spectators—and water down below to catch any flaming ashes. Those big dangerous fireworks went off in the middle of our street—mere feet from our home—for hours into the night. And not only on July 4 either. The celebrations took place the entire week. Each firework—with a noise eerily resembling the sound of a gunshot—would jolt us alert inside our house. My cheek clung to my fresh-out-of-the-freezer pillow, and my eyes were wide-awake wondering where in the world I was. I simply waited for the celebrations to cease and quiet to settle down on top of the city. People in Hamtramck sure did love America.

Ironically, living in the inner city had been a desire of mine throughout college. Back then I read books on overcoming poverty. I worked at inner-city camps. I wanted to live in less desirable neighborhoods for the sake of the gospel. I wanted to move somewhere unfamiliar and uncomfortable to bring comfort and blessing to others. This was the thing that had attracted me to Neil's online dating profile in the first place. He'd wanted to do this as well. Finally, here we were, living that out. And it was a lot harder than I'd thought it would be.

So many of the things I wanted most in life had been given to me. But things still weren't as I imagined they would be. I was married now, but this marriage didn't come with a white picket fence or a traditional three-bedroom home. Marriage didn't quite fulfill the longing for comfort and companionship like I thought it would. I was living in the middle of an inner city—a dream I had had in college—but it wasn't as fun as I hoped, or I wasn't as adventurous as I once had been. City living didn't quite fulfill the desire I had to make a difference in the world. I had a sweet little baby, but this baby didn't sleep well, and I was so tired. Being a mama wasn't as glamorous or full of lullabies and bedtime stories as I had imagined.

I seemed to have gotten everything I asked for and then found myself not wanting those things anymore! What do I do then? Throw the gifts away? Turn around and find something else shiny and sparkly and new? Or maybe I pause the inner temper tantrum and dig in deep to what God has for me here. I remind myself that while God's plan may look different from what I originally envisioned, his plan and his path are always better than what I could dream up. While I desire a final destination, he wants me to find joy in the journey. He has a purpose in his plans. And the longing for something more that I still feel even after I have been given what I asked for is a reminder that I cannot fill those empty spaces in my soul with dreams or wishes. Only God can fill them. And he provides a deep satisfaction in living life under his charge and gives me a longing for more of him.

|||||||||||||||||||||||||||||||||||||||||||||||||||||||||||||||||||||||||||||||||

And so while it wasn't my original plan, Hamtramck was where I found myself. In Hamtramck, no one assumes you are from America. Everyone guesses which country you must be from on the basis of your dress, language, and appearance. Neil and I having no recent country to call our own outside the United States was appalling and confusing to most of our neighbors. We almost started telling everyone that we'd just arrived here from Germany or Ireland in order to fit in a bit more.

There was no Target or Starbucks within twenty-five minutes of where we lived. And no chain restaurants besides

McDonald's and Wendy's—and even those closed down less than three years after we moved to Hamtramck. When you drive off the interstate and enter the city limits of Hamtramck, you are met with a restaurant on the right that serves Mexican, Chinese, and gyros—claiming to be good at all three. Maybe it really is.

Driving a little farther, you stumble upon a hipster live local theater building. Its marquee advertises improv classes, live music, and weekly comedy variety shows. The local mosque comes next, sending its call to prayer over the loudspeaker five times a day. Swarms of men and boys enter and exit those doors on Friday around noon to take part in the Islamic practice of Jumu'ah, a weekly congregational prayer.

Crossing over the main street of Hamtramck, you see cheap dollar stores and locally owned corner stores selling cigarettes, kitchen items, and flip-flops—a plethora of items that don't really make sense together. The boxes of the eight-piece place setting and the off-brand doll on display are faded and torn from sitting in the window year after year.

The post office and bank stand out among the rest. They are beautiful and built to last—their brick designs and inlays holding so much history. Looking at those buildings, you can catch a glimpse of what Hamtramck used to be in its glory days—bustling, busy, and full of life. Today it still looks busy, but the life isn't so fresh and new. Buildings are crumbling, people look tired, and the sidewalks that were once new and smooth are now cracked and crooked.

There are over forty bars in our small city, with bands traveling from out of state to play at them each weekend. The music scene is big here, as is the number per capita of liquor stores. The strangest one is the Corner Party Store, which we have nicknamed "Tall Shelves." The shelves literally reach from floor to ceiling and are packed with every type of alcohol, expired candy, socks, cigarettes, frozen pizza, and ancient phone chargers—but also the best selection of Ben & Jerry's ice cream. The restaurants make and serve authentic Bengali and Lebanese cuisine, the smell of their unique spices wafting through the air. Ride shares pull up to neighbors' homes and honk at early hours to pick people up for their shift on the car manufacturing lines at General Motors.

It's a blue-collar, hardworking, small urban town with dirt and weeds and various languages and cultures all trying to come together to make a community work. I was used to clean sidewalks, well-kept lawns, two-car garages, and cul-de-sacs filled with kids riding their bikes. This was a different culture—and I wasn't a part of it.

I felt like the biggest fish out of water. I didn't belong, I couldn't breathe, and I was grasping for something familiar to hold on to. So to cope, I left the uncomfortable and ran to something safe. Every day, I'd strap Jonah into his car seat and leave the city. We'd drive twenty-five minutes north on I-75 to Barnes & Noble and play at the train table set. Or I'd drive twenty-five minutes west on I-96 to wander the aisles of Target—before it was a trendy thing to do. Or we'd hang out at the mall, thanks to its air conditioning and its familiar stores such as Gap, Old Navy, and Carter's.

I remember driving out of my blighted neighborhood, traveling thirty minutes down the road, cresting the top of a hill, and coming down into modern suburbia. Flowers hung from street lights and paved the way to Starbucks. The Hallelujah chorus might as well have played, because every time I left Hamtramck and went back to middle-class America—even just for the day—I felt at home. I felt safe. I felt known. I was certain that Hamtramck could never be that for me. It was impossible.

I told Neil that one night. Despite our best intentions of moving to this city to make connections and friends with people of different cultures and backgrounds, I now realized it wasn't going to work. I would never become friends with even one of my neighbors. I was sorry, but we had made a huge mistake, and we needed to leave.

Neil somehow mustered up enough grace and compassion not to pick a fight with me in that moment. Instead, he pulled out the biggest—and possibly the most dangerous—weapon he had in his toolbelt. The Bible. And he turned to the book of Jonah. When he asked me to read a couple of verses but to replace Jonah's name with mine, I looked at him as if he had just swallowed a frog—or maybe been swallowed by a whale. Was he really pulling out the Bible in this moment? The moment I told him that things weren't working out so great in Hamtramck?

Yes, yes, he was. But he seemed so earnest and so eager, and he was being so tender, so I read it. Aloud.

The passage I read (Jonah 1:1–3) basically could have been translated this way: "The Lord gave this message to Rebecca: 'Get up and go to the great city of Hamtramck...' But Rebecca got up and went in the opposite direction to get away from the Lord. She went down the interstate to Canton, where she found a Target that looked nice and shiny. She bought some coffee at Starbucks, hoping to escape from the Lord."

If you aren't familiar with the story of Jonah, it doesn't end well for him. He ends up being thrown off the ship he boarded to avoid going to the city God told him to go to and gets swallowed by a whale—or a big fish. (The jury's still out on that technicality.) When he gets out of that fish belly—I assume similar to the way Pinocchio did—God tells him to go back. Go back to the city he told Jonah to go to in the first place.

So Jonah does, probably with his head hung low and sulking as he went. He's dragging his feet in the dirt, but he obeys. He tells the people of Nineveh to repent, and they do. The whole city ends up turning away from their wickedness and toward God. God wanted to use Jonah. Sure, he could have probably waved a magic wand and turned the people's hearts toward himself. Or he could have chosen to use someone else when Jonah protested, but he wanted to change Jonah's heart too, and he wanted to do it by sending him to a city filled with people whom Jonah didn't like.

I had found myself in a situation I didn't like. In a place that felt uncomfortable and hard. Why couldn't I have been sent to Hawaii instead of Hamtramck? Why isn't God more compassionate, and why doesn't he always send us to comfortable places? What was I going to do? Was I going to run from this city and this place because it felt too hard, too scary, too uncomfortable? Or was I going to dig deep and actually start living in the place where I went to sleep each night? What if I chose to start walking the sidewalks of this city? Shopped at the markets here? Said hi to the people I passed on the street? What if I stayed and stuck it out? What if God had something big planned here that I would get to be a part of only if I stayed? What if staying was part of that plan, even though staying seemed too hard?

I had been running from Hamtramck because it was strange and uncomfortable. I felt like a square peg trying to squeeze myself into a round hole, and those sharp edges and corners hurt—a lot. We feel so much more motivated to run to places of comfort when something is poking at our sides, don't we? We want that poking, squeezing feeling to stop because it hurts! I mean, when I find myself trying to follow a low-carb, no-sugar diet, there's nothing I'd rather eat than a big piece of chocolate cake with a huge scoop of ice cream, even though I know the right choice is protein and veggies. When my marriage was in a season of hardship, it seemed easier to consider divorce than it did to stay and figure it out. And when parenting small children starts to suffocate the life out of me, I am tempted to turn on the TV and let Sesame Street and Elmo babysit my kids so I don't have to spend the energy entertaining and breaking up fights.

But running away isn't the answer to soothing our hurting hearts. Pain and being uncomfortable are not the enemy. They are often the tools God uses to heal us and make us whole. Maybe I needed to stay uncomfortable long enough for God to smooth out my square edges. Maybe I needed to decide that I did fit in here—and to start calling Hamtramck my home. Maybe if I did, I might like it here.

So I tried it. I tested out the cheesy saying my mom always threw in my direction when life was hard-ish—bloom where you're planted. I sure hadn't dreamed of living here. This wasn't my original dream of the white picket fence. It didn't seem fair that I had to raise my baby in this dirty, dangerous, dilapidated place. But this is where I found myself. I had been planted in this garden filled with weeds and overgrown with shrubbery instead of blooming with the lilacs and peonies I preferred. Even if I didn't want to be here, I could at least try to bloom amid the hardness and see what beauty I could bring to the landscape of Hamtramck.

I'm not saying it was easy. I still hated most every day here. Growing roots was hard work. And my interactions with my neighbors and the women at the grocery store were awkward at best. But I was showing up. I wasn't running away. And that was something.

The more I stayed in Hamtramck, the more of its blight

and dirt I noticed. I wished it wasn't this way. I wanted my story to be pretty. I wanted to immediately fall in love with the old brick buildings and the crooked sidewalks and the sounds of the church bells quarreling with the haunting sound of the Muslim call to prayer. This would come, but not for a few more years.

I still woke up each day hoping and believing that God would do as he'd promised—that if I stayed, he would show me beauty and purpose in living here. I just wished he would hurry up!

| | | | | | | | | | | | | | | | | | | | | | | | | | | | | | | | | | | | | | | | | | | | | | | |

Out of everything I saw in Hamtramck, I especially hated the abandoned home that was falling down next to our house. I imagined drug dealers and homeless men taking up residence under its paper-thin roof or—perhaps even worse—my kids stepping on rusty nails, or crumbling walls falling down on them as they played with chalk on the sidewalk out front.

I had to look at that abandoned house next to our rental multiple times every single day. And each time I saw it, I wished it were gone. No matter what work I did to fix the home we lived in, such as planting flowers or painting the porch, that abandoned home stood there as a reminder of where I lived. The roof was caving in, the windows were boarded up, and on top of the graffiti marking its walls was a giant orange sign declaring the home unlivable—as if its appearance alone didn't make that obvious.

I hated that abandoned house. And I hated that I had to live next door to it. I hated that I had to raise my kids next door to a place that invited rats and squatters and decay. I wanted it gone.

Our neighbor's daughter had recently been hit by a car while she played on the sidewalk in front of her house, and I was sick of the lack of green space and safe areas for kids to play. I imagined how fun it would be to have a park right next to my home instead of the abandoned house. As Jonah got bigger, I longed for a big backyard for him to play in. The backyard of our rental house wasn't even big enough for a swing. If someone came to tear down this falling-down house, we would have space to put up a swing set and a slide.

I didn't fast or pray for hours about this. It wasn't something I even thought to ask God about. I figured he had bigger and more important things to do than help me tear down an old abandoned house next door. After all, I had been asking God to help me fit in to Hamtramck. I didn't think he would change Hamtramck to fit me and my desires. This abandoned house was part of Hamtramck—something I needed to learn to deal with—and even love.

Day after day, I would walk outside our home, look to the left, and still see that abandoned home wasting away, a dismal reminder that this place God had called me to was nothing like the neighborhood I dreamed of raising a family in. Day after day, I would push Jonah in a stroller around Hamtramck, just waiting for the day when I would learn to love it.

One morning, I woke up to a lot of noise outside. Jonah and I ran to the hallway window of our second-story apartment, and my mouth fell open. I sprinted to get my camera so I could document the miraculous sight outside.

We watched, transfixed, as an excavator, completely destroying the sidewalk with the weight of its wheels, tore down the abandoned house like Cookie Monster wolfing down a box of cookies. The strength of its scoop breaking through the roof and walls was impressive. Its long arm reached right past our window to grab at more house, and I gasped as I read the black letters painted on the side of its giant yellow arm: A-B-L-E.

Tears pooled in the corners of my eyes as I heard God whisper that he is able. Able to hear my dreams and wishes and hopes even when I didn't set aside hours a day to talk to him about them. Able to act in big and powerful ways for a seemingly small girl in the middle of Detroit who just wanted the abandoned house next to her torn down. Able not only to change my heart to love a city but to change a city to become more loveable. He was able. He is able. He sees our dreams and our desires. He has good plans for us, and they probably include the things we want most. And he will complete them and see them finished—even when we don't know what to ask for or how to move forward.

He sees. He sees your tears at night when no one else is awake. He cares. He cares for the deepest desires of your heart—the ones you've never shared with a single soul. And he acts. He acts on our behalf and for our good.

What if I had been gone that day? What if I had woken up that day and left the city limits of Hamtramck for the suburban comfort of Target and Starbucks? What if I hadn't stayed? I would have missed the wonderful miracle of this excavator named Able coming to rescue me from the abandoned house next door.

By choosing to stay in the dirt and the mud and the blight, we get a front-row seat to the beautiful change of God making things new. But to see it happen, we have to stay. We have to stand in the mud to see blight exchanged for beauty.

CHAPTER 3

Notice the Small Beginnings

Because Everything—Literally Everything—Starts Small

||||||||||||||||||||||||||||||||||||||||||||||||||||||||||||||||||||||||

I was introduced to Nadia soon after my decision to stop running away from Hamtramck. She was my age and was born in Texas while her dad was on a student visa—granting her American citizenship—but spent the rest of her childhood in Yemen. After her arranged marriage at age sixteen, Nadia and her husband moved to Hamtramck, along with her father. They had lived here for ten years and had three older girls and a boy about Jonah's age. Because so many languages are spoken in Hamtramck, there's no need to learn fluent English, and Nadia hadn't. So when Nadia's father, who had recently met my husband, asked whether Nadia could come visit our home to meet me, I hesitated. What would I talk to her about? How would I talk to her?

"She sews," Neil said, trying to convince me to step out of

my comfort zone and meet someone living in Hamtramck. I had been given a sewing machine a year earlier for my birthday and had been enjoying this new hobby.

"Fine." I sighed. "Invite her over."

We arranged a time for her to bring her four children over to my home at a time when Neil was gone. In her culture, being in the same room with a man that isn't a part of your family is forbidden.

Neil kissed me goodbye at the door thirty minutes before she was to arrive.

"Good luck," he said with a wink. "You'll do great. Just be yourself."

But I was a nervous wreck, trying to hold in embarrassing hot tears from pouring out as I gave myself internal pep talks, and kissed him back.

This is just a woman. A short meeting. A little get-together. You can do this.

I didn't know what women from Yemen ate or what they liked to drink. I knew she would probably come dressed in her black abaya with her face covered. Did she expect that of me too? Would she take it off when she got inside? What would she be wearing underneath? What if my house was too warm? What if Jonah was tired and needed a nap? What if I was tired and wanted her to go home?

When she arrived, I put on my happy face. She couldn't see through to the fear. But after twenty minutes of sitting awkwardly in my dusty and dark living room and wanting to die a figurative death, I gestured to Nadia to follow me to an even dustier and darker part of the house—our basement. It was where I had set up the very small, very new Etsy shop I had started just a few months before.

I was making bags, custom ones that allowed the customer

(mostly my friends at this point) to pick out the fabric and design the bag to their own style and liking. It had all started when I made a diaper bag for myself while Neil was overseas on his vision trip to China. I was home alone—bored, nesting, and worried because of the lack of communication during the riot that had shut the internet down from thousands of miles away. Sewing kept my hands busy and my mind occupied until Neil could call to tell me he was okay.

For three days in a row, I dragged my new sewing machine over to a friend's house, and she showed me step-by-step how to sew a bag. I was proud of our work and excited to pack the bag full of diapers and onesies and rattles soon. Picking out the coordinating fabrics had been so fun, and I loved how the cream daisies popped against the dark brown background of the bag's base. The flap was a mint green polka-dot print and had a dark brown ribbon sewn across with a bow.

After making that first diaper bag, I posted pictures of it on Facebook and got lots of comments from friends asking me whether I had thought about selling them on Etsy. I had never even heard of this Etsy thing. Apparently, it was a new website that had recently launched into internet land that allowed you to open your own online shop and sell handmade products. I typed Etsy.com into my search bar and clicked "Register." All I needed to get started was an email address and a shop name.

I looked around my bedroom for inspiration. Becky's Bags? Becky's Beautiful Bags? I've always had a soft spot for alliteration. Then my eyes landed on a gift card peeking out under piles of bills, receipts, and ultrasound pictures on my desk. It was a twenty-five-dollar gift card for Kiva.org that my progressive brother had given me the previous Christmas. Kiva is an amazing microloan website where anyone can hop on and send microloans to people in Third World countries. I thought it was a terrible Christmas gift at the time. I had been given twenty-five bucks that I couldn't even spend on myself. Eventually I would get it back—when the loan was repaid—but I first had to launder it through someone in a Third World country who was trying to buy sheep.

As it would turn out, my brother nailed the Christmas gift game. I loved searching the hundreds of profiles of men and women who were trying to start or grow their own businesses overseas. All that was standing in their way was the financial resources to do so. And I got to decide whom I would send my first twenty-five-dollar microloan to. I chose Ergashali from Tajikistan. He had six children and a wife and needed one thousand dollars to buy more cattle for his farm. So I joined Cammie from Junction City, Steven from London, Joseph from Corona, Dianne from New York, and thirty-two others from around the world, each of us loaning around twenty-five dollars to collectively add up to what Ergashali needed to buy more cows. Ergashali paid us back over the next fourteen months, and I had already found another person to loan more money to a week later.

I had an idea. I could sign up for an Etsy shop, sell these bags like my friends wanted me to, and loan money to more people using part of the sales from the bags. And maybe I could send a picture of the person the loan was going to with the bag so my friends could feel involved in the process too. We were going to make a lot of lives better—one bag at a time.

So I typed in the box labeled "Shop Name": Better Life Bags.

|||||||| |||||||| |||||||||||||||||||||||||||||||||||||||||||||||||||||||||||||||||||||||||

Nadia and I spent a few hours in the basement making bags together that night. It wasn't life-changing, but it was obedient.

God had asked me to stay—to quit running to the surrounding suburbs and start meeting people in my city—and here I was, trying to do that. I was interacting with and becoming involved in the lives of the people who lived here. I couldn't for the life of me figure out how this encounter in the basement, where neither Nadia nor I could understand each other, would or could ever be used by God, but I had committed to this little experiment of not running away. I had committed to staying and seeing what would happen—what this big God Thing might be—if I remained where he had planted me and got down close to the ground to dig my roots in deep.

The thing about digging your roots in deep is that it requires staying still. It starts with small roots that don't look like much of anything, and you aren't even sure they are worth growing. But you choose to stay—day after day—and the roots grow deeper and wider into the soil until they stabilize and become secure enough for the flower to grow taller and eventually bloom.

Did you know that the roots of trees and plants spread to more than two times the size of what you see above the soil? What you see is only a fraction of what is going on under the surface. Invisible to the eye and growing bigger than the tree itself, strong roots have worked their way through the soil and provided a strong foundation for the tree to grow taller and spread its branches further. What's more amazing is that the entire spectacle started as a tiny seed that could fit in the palm of your hand.

Looking back ten years later, I can see that awkward encounter in the basement as the planting of a small seed. I didn't know it then, but this small act of obedience—agreeing to meet a woman from Hamtramck—would soon take root and give Better Life Bags the foundation it needed to spring up from the soil. I think that's how it goes with most small beginnings. We don't even know they are the beginning of something until we've gone a bit down the road and turn and look back. It's then that we notice where we came from and what got us there along the way.

Not knowing the huge role Nadia would play in the life of Better Life Bags, I'm ashamed—and feel a little guilty—to say I never called Nadia again after that night. Not for quite a few years. It had been an awkward encounter, and I wasn't eager to relive it. But something happened thirty-six months later that forced me to dig into my phone contacts for her number.

I was going to need her help. Desperately.

| | | | | | | | | | | | | | | | | | | | | | | | | | | | | | | | | | | | | | | | | | | | | | | | | | | | | | | | | | | | | | | | | | | | | | | | |

I didn't know what to do to make Better Life Bags grow, but I knew I had to do something. My small hobby had grown a little bit. It was teetering on the line between a fun little side gig and a super-small business. Neil was the first to point this out to me. We were supposed to be on a breakfast date at Panera. He sat me down over a hot mocha and an Asiago-cheese bagel and whipped out a pen and a napkin. I quickly realized this wasn't going to be the romantic morning date I had envisioned. He started mapping out how many hours I had been spending on work, even though I barely would have called it work at this point. I mean, I was sewing and selling bags and blogging and figuring out Instagram. That was all fun! A creative little hobby! What was the problem?

Well, the problem was that I wasn't making much money. I was spending a lot of time sewing bags—before Jonah woke up in the morning, during his naptimes, and after he went to bed. And during any of his awake times, I was Instagramming, emailing customers, and planning new bag designs in my head. All of this was fun! I would never have called it work. But Neil was right. After he calculated it all out, I realized I was making somewhere around twenty-five cents per hour. This hobby-looking thing was starting to grow a little faster than I was prepared for. More and more people were discovering my Etsy shop each week.

Until recently, I had been able to keep up with the orders streaming in, but lately, I had needed Neil's help keeping Jonah entertained so I could catch up with sewing—especially as he grew into a toddler and needed constant supervision. Our family also needed to make a personal decision. Our salary with the nonprofit we moved up to Michigan with was no longer enough for our family to live on. I never felt as though we were in need, but our year-end taxes showed us living well below the poverty level. We humbly used food stamps to buy groceries and were grateful for state-provided healthcare to cover pregnancies, births, and well-child checkups. But we didn't want to live like this forever. We needed to find something else to boost us out of poverty. I wondered whether Better Life Bags could do that for us. I needed to either figure out whether this sewing thing could actually make money, or I needed to be done—or at least severely scale it back so Neil could find another full-time job with a higher paying salary.

Knowing that I didn't want this fun, creative outlet of mine to be over for good, I asked Neil for six months to see whether Better Life Bags could provide significantly for our family, and I got to work. I listened to Amy Porterfield tell me how to run a successful Facebook campaign. I read books about how to price your product for profit and later raised my prices—and no one seemed to care or even notice. I observed how other companies sent free product to bloggers in exchange for exposure and publicity, and I did the same.

I attended Blissdom, a conference in Dallas, Texas, for creative bloggers and business owners, where I set up a table and sold my bags. My Better Life Bags table was set up right between two powerhouses in the online product world: The Shine Project and Lisa Leonard Designs. I was able to pick their brains on what works and how to generate more online sales. I also shared a room with Kate Bryan, a beauty blogger from The Small Things blog. She would end up being a huge support and cheerleader for Better Life Bags.

In early 2013 blogs were starting to explode. I knew being featured on a blog was a free and quick way to be seen by lots of people. So I marketed to potential customers through the blogging world. My first attempts at this failed. I was only familiar with the blogging world of do-it-yourselfers and sent bags to these crafty mamas to host giveaways on their blogs. But most everyone reading the posts and entering the giveaways really only wanted to figure out how to make my bags themselves, not buy them.

So when I was at Blissdom and met Kate, someone completely outside the crafty blog niche, I asked whether I could send her a bag to review. She designed a Molly bag—the cute, boxy, everyday crossbody style—and when the blog post went live, I sold blue-and-white herringbone Mollys for weeks afterward. I'm forever grateful.

In hopes of continuing to sell enough bags to bring the business into the black, I knew I needed even more exposure. I had heard about another conference a few hundred miles from my house that would bring hundreds of Christian women together and had a boutique where women could sell their handmade goods. Without hesitation, I signed up.

I also figured out who all the speakers and leaders at the conference would be and emailed them to see whether I could make them bags to carry around at the conference. They could be walking advertisements for Better Life Bags!

Two of the leaders who would be facilitating a small breakout session at the conference got overly excited about designing their bags. They must have been texting each other about possible design options because I suddenly heard from both at almost the same time.

"Rebecca!" one email read, "We absolutely love your bags and would be thrilled to carry one around at the conference coming up! Just one question—have you ever thought about adding leather somehow to the bags? Maybe a leather strap? Or a leather flap? Not sure if it's possible, but I'd love a Brynnda bag with some leather added in. Let us know what you think!"

I had never worked with leather before. All my bags up until that point had been made of 100 percent cotton fabric. I didn't even know where to buy leather. I assumed you'd probably need a dairy farm to have access to cows because leather came from cows. (Or at least I thought it did.)

After a bit of googling, I found a store thirty minutes away that sold leather. I decided to head that direction to buy a yard of leather to test out whether my sewing machine could handle the thickness of this new material.

The next day, I pulled up to Tandy Leather and pushed against the front door. The trio of bells hanging from the doorknob clattered against the glass as I entered. It smelled glorious, almost as good as the bike aisle at Walmart.

Not even knowing where to start—and a little nervous to be there—I started walking up and down aisles of various shades of brown and black leather hides, pretending to know what I was looking for. My fingers ran across the smooth and buttery sides, stopping to finger the scars and brands littered over the hides. This was once an actual cow. The thought was equally as surprising as it was obvious. I had no idea what I was doing or what type of leather I was looking for, so I timidly approached the guy at the counter. Wiry and graying, he was partially hidden behind a rugged beard. His leather vest and tattooed arms weren't helping me feel as if I fit in, but I figured he was getting paid to help customers, and right now I fit that description.

"I need a yard of leather, please," I said quietly, feeling small as he towered over me.

He laughed. This wasn't good. That wasn't the response I'd been hoping for.

It turned out that you couldn't buy just a yard of leather. You had to buy the whole cow. And the whole cow wasn't cheap. You could easily drop hundreds of dollars, depending on the style, weight, and finish of the leather. There was a lot to learn here, and I had to decide whether I was going to spend a month's earnings on an entire cowhide of leather—just to make two people bags for free in hopes that others would see them and want one too.

That seems crazy, right? But I had a feeling this leather suggestion might be my next special sticker—my next step in this journey. I was going to follow it until it didn't lead anywhere, until I hit a dead end. This didn't seem to be a dead end, so I bought the whole cow.

I was sweating as I picked out the cowhide I wanted—a beautiful, distressed, worn-in looking brown hide that the guy up front assured me was the perfect weight for my sewing machine. It was the type of leather you would use on a couch or chair, unlike the thicker kind used for chaps and buckles, which this store also sold if I ever considered changing the name of my shop to Better Life Belts.

I walked out of the leather store carrying an entire cow

draped over my shoulder. This better pay off, I thought as I threw the leather hide across the back seat of my Toyota Camry. I also knew all too well that if it did work, I would have to show my face here again and be forever known as the woman who'd asked to buy a yard of leather.

I rushed home and couldn't wait to get that leather under my sewing machine to see how it worked. The handheld rotary blade I used to cut fabric glided nicely through the leather hide, cutting the pattern pieces out with ease. I sat down at the sewing machine and lined up a piece of square fabric on top of a piece of leather the same size and shape. I was going to try making the flap with leather on the front and a fabric as the lining. My foot cautiously pushed down on the pedal—I didn't want to accelerate too fast—and the needle pressed slowly down into the hide. I pushed a little harder on the pedal, and a few more stitches came together. The needle was gliding up and down through the fabric and leather layers like butter. When the flap was done, I lifted the sewing machine foot, pulled out the married-together squares, and cut the thread holding them to the sewing machine. The texture of the leather next to the color of the fabric was stunning and unlike anything I had seen in the market.

I couldn't wait to get these bags into the hands of the conference leaders. I rushed to make a few more leather and fabric bags to have for sale at the conference market, but as I posted pictures and sneak peeks on Instagram of what I was making, all the bags sold before the conference even started. So at the conference, I arranged a few in-person design-your-own-bag sessions. I took fabric samples and a leather swatch and sat down in the corner of the conference market three times during the course of the weekend to design bags with conference attendees. They had all seen these leather and fabric bags being carried around and wanted one for themselves. And the experience of getting to design your own bag was truly something new and exciting.

I arrived home from that conference excited and eager to make more bags but also needing more leather. I found myself visiting that leather store so often that everyone there learned my name. When I wasn't cutting leather or fabric, I was sewing bags together. And if I wasn't sewing bags together, I was shipping orders out to customers. If I wasn't shipping orders to customers, I was answering design questions via email. And if I wasn't answering emails, I was playing around on a new website called Pinterest.

Pinterest started as a fun and mindless activity for me. I'd use it instead of Google to search for images and ideas for crafts or recipes or fashion, then pin the ones I liked to my own organized boards to save for later. I could search "Valentine crafts" and see images of hundreds and hundreds of craft ideas and tutorials. A search for "leather sandals" would give me a seemingly endless number of clickable links to purchase from.

I realized how much fun I was having pinning shirts and shoes and necklaces from other online companies as I created my own Pinterest boards. I thought it might be a good idea for my little Etsy shop if I pinned Better Life Bags on a Pinterest board of its own! Maybe someone would stumble upon my bags and click the link to my website, just as I was clicking links to other people's products!

A couple of days after pinning our bags to Pinterest, I got this text from a friend:

> OMG, Rebecca. Joy Cho just repinned a Better Life Bag to her Pinterest board. She's like SO famous in the blogging world! Ok that's all. Just thought you should know.

Another sticker. Another gift from God—this time in the form of free marketing exposure. It was time for Better Life Bags to grow a little more.

The Joy Cho Pinterest moment was one of the first and one of the biggest organic marketing moments for Better Life Bags. Joy Cho had over three million Pinterest followers at the time—six million eager eyes watching and wanting every item she pinned, six million eyes that saw our black-and-white striped fabric and leather laptop bag and instantly wanted it—and clicked over to the Better Life Bags shop.

I'm not sure the bag would have caught Joy Cho's eye if it had been all fabric. Anyone could make an all-fabric bag. But the brown distressed leather next to the black-and-white striped fabric gave the bag an urban, modern feel that didn't look anything like a handmade bag. Adding leather set us apart from every other bag company on Etsy. Over the next ten years, we would move to making entire bags out of leather, as well as adding lots of colors of leather to our line. In fact, leather became the backbone of our company—a distinct feature of Better Life Bags—and it started with one small request.

God used those two customers asking about leather to create the core of our company's brand without me even realizing it. And he used my small and fearful but brave steps into the leather store to grow my company. I had been faithful with the small things, and now he was giving me bigger things—new materials to work with and a bigger audience. I had been faithful to buckle down and do the work and take the risks required to turn my twenty-five cents per hour wage into something more substantial, and he was rewarding my efforts.

Those first two bags made with leather hold a special place in my heart. They were the tangible results of taking a risk. Knowing how important this moment was for me and my company, a friend had a keychain made for me. Engraved on the side were the words "Buy the Whole Cow," and it hangs on my bulletin board to this day—reminding me that sometimes we need to take small steps with big risks to see great growth. Sometimes we need to invest in the whole cow.

|||||||||||||||||||||||||||||||||||||||||||||||||||||||||||||||||||||||||

Orders came in faster than I could fill them. Everyone seemed to love this new design feature, and our sales more than doubled. I had two babies by this point. Sweet little Clara Lynn had joined our family just fifteen short months after her big brother, Jonah, was born. I was wrangling babies on two hips while sewing bags with two hands. I needed help.

At this point a lot of people told me to close the shop—call it a fun few years. How was I going to be a mom of two and keep up with all these orders? Our bedroom had been moved into the living room to make more space for the bags, except they weren't staying contained in that small corner room. Bags were piling up all around our house.

Molly bags had commandeered our couch, thanks to Kate's blog post. The kitchen table had been cleared off to make room for two high school gals who were helping me sort fabric scraps. Claire, a girl in my local Bible study, started babysitting for me so I could have uninterrupted time to make more bags. And her mom, Elise, who would eventually become our operations manager, was volunteering her time by using a tiny table shoved up against the kitchen window to sew hundreds of long leather straps for all these orders. Jonah, two years old by then, ran by one time and accidentally stepped on the sewing pedal, and the machine took off in a whirlwind. We laughed because that was exactly how we felt inside—chaotic and frantic and running around, trying to bust out bags as fast as we could. But it still wasn't fast enough.

I couldn't keep up and keep my sanity.

I realized I couldn't do this all myself, not even with the little bit of help I had around me. In a moment of desperation, I remembered Nadia. I remembered how we had tried to get acquainted in that dark and dingy basement, not able to communicate beyond the universal language of the sewing machine. But she was the only person I knew who might be able to help me dig myself out from under the mountain of bags. I still had her number in my phone—originally put in there as a courtesy, as I never thought I'd actually call and want to get together. But I needed her now.

My palms were sweating as I tapped out the number on my phone. "Dialing Nadia . . ."

"Please know more English. . . . Please be able to understand me . . ." I whispered under my breath as the phone rang.

"Hello?" a voice answered.

"Nadia! This is Rebecca. Do you remember me? We sewed together in my basement a year or so ago."

I breathed a deep sigh of relief when Nadia confirmed that she did remember me. And she spoke wonderful English—something she'd learned by watching cartoons every day while her girls were at school. I explained that I needed help making bags and wanted to come over and teach her how to make the insides of the bags so I could make the outsides. Together we could sew them twice as fast.

Within a week, I packed up my two kids along with my sewing machine and fabric and found myself in Nadia's living room. I had hesitated at the door before I knocked. This seemed to be a terrible idea. We didn't really know each other. Would I come across as needy by asking for help? Would she even be able to sew with leather? Was God using Better Life Bags and our overwhelming orders to push me to connect with Nadia?

I couldn't be sure what the plan was, but Nadia was my only hope for help and relief. So I knocked. Her daughter cracked the door to see who it was, then flung it open wide. I walked in to the smell of burning incense and mint tea. Within minutes, I was embraced in one of Nadia's big hugs that I would become so familiar with over the next seven years. She asked me to sit and handed me tea. My children got busy playing with toys and eating lollipops fetched from the corner gas station before we arrived. Nadia joined me on the couch with her cup of tea and a smile. Here we were. And here I was, sitting next to one of my neighbors in her home, something I never thought was possible.

When I had lamented to Neil that night early in our life in Hamtramck that I would never be friends with any of my neighbors, I couldn't see how I would have anything in common with someone who wasn't a white, middle-class American like I was. It's embarrassing to admit, but it's true. But what I was discovering while getting to know Nadia in her home was that under her black abaya, she wore jeans and a tank top just like I did. She was a mom—just like I was. Hamtramck was new for her—just like it was for me. And while that first encounter in my living room three years before was awkward and uncomfortable, this time we had a reason to meet. We had something to talk about and connect over—the bags. We had a common goal and something we were both working toward together. Instead of an uncomfortable first date, this felt as if we were teammates.

I didn't know why God asked me to stop running and start digging into the soil of Hamtramck to create some roots and see what would bloom. I didn't know how he could use me in this city. But he knew. He knew if I stopped running and stayed around a little bit, I'd have time to make more bags. And those bags would grow and multiply so much that I would need to reach out to Nadia for help. This little Etsy shop might just be my purpose for living here. It had given me a reason to start a relationship and friendship with my neighbor, and I was hopefully expectant.

||||||||||||||||||||||||||||||||||||||||||||||||||||||||||||||||||||||||||

That day in her home, I taught Nadia to sew one of my bags. And we started this beautiful partnership and rhythm of meeting together each week to trade finished bags for more fabric to turn into more bags. Having Nadia on board as an employee with me now meant that my life could slow down a bit. The weight of making orders and sending them out on time didn't rest solely on my shoulders. I didn't have to use every naptime for bag-making anymore. Little by little, I taught Nadia more bags, and I dug myself out from underneath a pile of orders.

Better Life Bags had become a life-giving venture for me. It was fulfilling to be creative and design new bags. It was fun to blog and post on social media about our bags as well as other things that interested me. And it was especially motivating when I was able to draw from the business PayPal account to fund a date night or our entire month's rent. I was making something that people wanted, and they were helping to provide for my family in a financial way. I didn't want it to end, and Nadia filled the need that I had to keep Better Life Bags going. But what I hadn't planned on or anticipated was the need that Better Life Bags filled for her.

Every week, I would come to Nadia's house with my kids and more fabric. I'd walk into her freshly swept home and take my shoes off at the door, then struggle to bend over and take off my toddlers' shoes as well. I'd sit on Nadia's couch and sip fresh hot tea with mint leaves. We would talk about life in America—what's good and what's different. I'd ask her questions about Yemen and try to imagine her home there—a home made of cinder-block walls with an inner courtyard. Her mother taught her to sew in one of the upper rooms. We shared our wedding stories and pictures together. I asked a million questions about what it was like to have an arranged marriage. I tried to memorize the names of her eleven brothers and sisters in hopes that I would meet them one day. We'd laugh while watching our kids play tag in the backyard or jump from couch to couch in the living room. After an hour or so, I'd leave with a fresh batch of bags tucked under my arm and a smile on my face.

When the weather warmed up, I asked whether she would like to walk to the park with me and all our kids. I wasn't sure whether she was allowed to—I had heard dramatic stories about women from Yemen not being allowed to leave their homes without their husbands. But for Nadia, this was untrue. And so we walked the streets of Hamtramck together—me, a white American dressed in jeans and a tank top, and Nadia, a Yemeni American dressed similarly but underneath her dark abaya and head covering.

"What are you asking God for?" I asked her one day as we enjoyed the fresh spring air on our way to the park.

"Kitchen cabinets," Nadia replied without hesitation.

So I joined her in asking God for kitchen cabinets until, one day, he provided them—not out of thin air or from the hat of a magician but instead from a cabinet store with a good sale.

Nadia loved those cabinets and credited God with answering her prayer for them.

When the heat of the summer settled in and it became too hot to walk to the park, we would sit together on her couch and watch HGTV. One afternoon, Nadia and I were watching a show about a bakery that specialized in making cupcakes. The cupcake shop was celebrating its one thousandth sale. Nadia and I looked at each other and talked about how crazy it would be to reach one thousand bag sales! And then we started praying that God would get us there.

With our income climbing every few months, Neil and I had started looking for a house to buy. Housing prices were at an all-time low, and you could snatch up a decent home in Hamtramck for under $50,000. We still hoped to move overseas in a year or so, but buying a house with a mortgage less than our rent seemed like a smart move. We could always resell if we moved—hopefully for a higher price—or rent the home out while we were gone. I told Nadia I was praying for a house with a big backyard and stairs inside. You would think that stairs inside the four walls of a two-story home would be an easy ask. But not in Hamtramck. Most houses had been originally built as duplexes, so when they were converted to single family homes, the stairs to the second floor were left on the outside of the house. I wanted a true single-family home. And I wanted a big yard for my kids to run and play in, which seemed highly unlikely in our crowded urban area. I'd be lucky to find a five-foot by five-foot area of green grass to spread a blanket on for a picnic. A swing set was a pipe dream. I wasn't asking for a white picket fence anymore.

After a few months of Nadia and me praying together and working hard behind our sewing machines, Better Life Bags sold its one thousandth bag. Little did we know that that number would multiply by twelve in just four years. This was still our small beginning—even though it felt so big! I got the notification for our one thousandth order in my email the day I was set to visit Nadia. I couldn't wait to share the news with her. We had done it! God had done it!

I knocked on the door and blurted it out as soon as she welcomed me in. "We've sold one thousand bags!" I exclaimed with my hands in the air. A smile spread across her face as she simply remarked, "You know, when you pray, God listens to you."

So we prayed for the most impossible thing we could think of—that Nadia's mom and siblings would be able to immigrate from Yemen to the United States. It had seemed possible for a while as they inched their way through red tape and interviews and paperwork. But so many obstacles kept popping up: a new president, some closed borders, a terrible war in Yemen, declined visas, and costly lawyer fees. This prayer was our asking for a straight-up miracle. Only God could handle this one. And I didn't have much faith it could happen. But instead of worrying about how it would come to pass, we started praying. We didn't know what else to do, so we started there—with a simple prayer.

On one of my regular visits to her house for fabric exchanges, hot tea, and conversation, Nadia met me at the door with an excited look on her face. I chased her up the stairs—straining to keep up—as she made a big gesture toward her girls' bedroom, where her daughters all slept together on mattresses lining the floor. Except the mattresses were no longer down on the ground. In their place was a beautiful bunk bed set—full size on the bottom and twin on the top. The girls were giddy with smiles, swinging their legs back and forth as they dangled off the top bunk, and I gazed in with amazement.

Then Nadia led me to the kitchen, where she proudly showed me the first dining room table and chair set she'd ever owned.

"You bought all this with the money I've been giving you to make bags?" I asked.

"Yes!" she exclaimed.

I couldn't believe it. Nadia wasn't just helping me—the bags were helping her! This was her first job, and neither of us even knew it would turn into a job when I made that first phone call. The income she was bringing in had greatly contributed to the needs of their family, allowing them to purchase items such as bunk beds and a dining set. Eventually, they were able to move to a bigger home and buy a brand-new minivan for their growing family.

That day, as she handed me a stack of completed bags, Nadia's fingers caught the suede label with our company name etched into it.

"Better Life Bags," she read out loud as her fingers traced the letters. "That's really true for me, you know. My life has so much purpose now. I have something to get up for in the morning. Something to do for me. My life is better."

Mine was too.

I wanted Better Life Bags to grow as much as God wanted it to. I wanted to help as many women in Hamtramck with jobs as we could. I wanted this little company to have a big impact on the neighborhood and become a stable force for good. If the business worked and did really well, we could create more companies that could hire men and more women from Hamtramck. Or we could start franchises of Better Life Bags in other cities. The options and growth trajectory could be endless. The number of lives that could be changed was infinite.

But there were more than big and grand dreams. The dreams went deep and small too. This company could provide for my family and allow us to rise above the poverty level, own a home, and start saving, investing, and giving more money. It would allow my husband the flexibility to pursue things that mattered to him without feeling tied down to a job he didn't love, just to pay the bills. It could be a legacy that I pass down to my daughter or sons someday—a family business that continues to run fifty years later. And it could mean that the daughters of my employees become the first in their families to go to college and earn degrees because of the examples their mothers set of valuable work. All because I made a diaper bag, posted pictures of it on Facebook, and started an Etsy shop. Those were such small, ordinary moments in and of themselves but with such big, lasting results.

I drove home that night, and as my eyes landed on house after house, I wondered whether there were other women inside them who might need a little boost in their family income. How many women like Nadia were living here in Hamtramck? There were so many who were capable, intelligent, smart, and willing to work but unable to find employment because of language barriers, a lack of education, or simply the fact that their conservative culture didn't allow them to work in the presence of men. Sewing bags in the safety and comfort of their own homes seemed to be a perfect fit for women like her.

This could become really big. At this point, I didn't know that soon this business that started four years before as a small Etsy shop would give over 180 loans to men and women in thirty-nine countries. We would grow from $470 in bag sales in 2009 to well over six figures in 2013. Nadia would furnish her home and make a significant contribution to her family's finances. I would make enough money to completely replace our original income level and convince Neil to quit his job to run Better Life Bags with me for a season. All because I decided one day to just start. Starting can sometimes feel as if it is the biggest hurdle, but it's usually the easiest step. You don't need to know how it's going to end or even what you need to do next. You just need to start. Part of the fun of this better life journey is following the breadcrumbs—those special stickers—laid out for you on your path that will tell you where to go next. But to find them, you need to start walking. Don't worry about step five. Begin with step one, and start with what you have.

CHAPTER 4

Do Something That Matters

A Bag without a Mission Is Just Pieces of Fabric Sewn Together

|||||||||||||||||||||||||||||||||||||||||||||||||||||||||||||||||||||||||||||||||||||||||||

When my husband noticed that there were bags in every room of our house except the bathroom, he told me it was time to find a new place to run the business. Our children needed to be able to roam freely instead of being told not to touch all the pretty bags hanging from every chair and tabletop.

I posted on Facebook to see whether anyone knew of some commercial space available in town, and a local pastor reached out to offer us part of his congregation's building they weren't currently using. We were able to move in rent free for the first few months! What a blessing. Another small step forward. Another special sticker. We were following the breadcrumbs.

Moving day was exciting. The building was missing ceiling tiles, but I didn't care. We had space. Since we didn't have a ton of equipment, it took us only a few trips from our house to the new workshop to move everything over. My parents kept our kids for us for a long weekend so Neil and I could do it in one fell swoop. We even turned the now-empty Better Life Bags headquarters in our home into a playroom for the kids. Our home was ours again.

Now that Better Life Bags had a workshop space, we could think about hiring more women. I knew most of the women in our community would want to work from home, but having this open space to come together for interviews, trainings, and meetings would be so helpful.

I was excited to hire more women from Hamtramck to help us make more and more bags. So when it felt as though the time was right—when Nadia and I were about at our maximum level of orders—I reached out to a friend who was teaching English classes at the church next door to the Better Life Bags workshop. I asked her whether any of her students knew how to sew and whether they would be interested in a part-time job.

She had four interested ladies!

I had never interviewed anyone for a job, but I figured that I should at least bring all four women in for a tryout of sorts. I needed to see whether they really could sew. So I gathered supplies to teach them how to make our laptop bag—the one Joy Cho had pinned on Pinterest and still remained our current bestselling bag.

We gathered in our workshop space, and despite the language barrier, I was able to show them each step in the bag-making process and had them copy it on their own sewing machines. Like Nadia, all the women had some level of sewing experience before trying out. But I needed to teach them how to make my bag designs. They all followed along with the instructions beautifully. How was I supposed to choose only one woman for the job? It was impossible, so I hired all four.

Soon another woman from the same English class joined our Better Life Bags team, and now we had six women sewing bags. In the process, I was slowly stepping away from the sewing and stepping into the role of working on the business— new bag designs, marketing, social media, and customer emails. I loved that aspect of the business. I especially loved crunching numbers and pricing our products in a way that would allow us to pay our ladies well and make a profit that we could put back into the business and use to hire even more women. And honestly, I was glad to hand off the sewing to others. Something that had started as my hobby had quickly turned into my job, and I was a bit tired of sewing.

We were still giving 10 percent of every sale through Kiva to a woman in a Third World country trying to start or grow a business of her own. I was astounded by how much money we had been able to give, and I was blogging about each woman we loaned money to so I could keep our growing Better Life Bags community updated.

While I loved giving out the loans and blogging about the recipients, I was realizing that the women making the bags for our customers had amazing stories of their own. Slowly, we started shifting away from making lives better for women thousands of miles away to making lives better for the women who lived in our own neighborhood. Instead of sending money overseas to someone we would never meet, we began to invest creatively in the lives of people we could see, touch, and hug on a daily basis—our employees.

We were running a full-fledged operation at this point, making meaningful work for women in our neighborhood. Sewing machines hummed along from nine to five. A few high school girls from the community chatted over the Pandora playlist while they cut fabric and leather to batch together for the seamstresses, who would walk through the door to drop off finished bags and pick up their next batch. Shipping bags to customers had become a full-time job, so I hired another friend, and we even had an intern from a local college apply to come help during the summer hours.

At this point, I wasn't sure that I could continue calling this bag company my hobby anymore. Under the IRS rules (loosely translated), a hobby turns into a business when you are actively trying to make a profit. According to my basic accounting software that helped me track income and expenses, it looked as though we would make more money than we would spend—the very definition of profit. It was time to make Better Life Bags an official business. We probably should have done this a year or so before, but when a hobby suddenly grows into a business, you start realizing all the legalities you need to abide by and start playing catch-up. So I found an accountant who helped start the process for us to become a corporation. Her first question to me when we sat down across from each other at the tiny round table at the coffee shop down the street was, "Do you want to be a nonprofit?"

So many people assumed we were a nonprofit. We were doing the work and had the mission of a typical nonprofit—to provide meaningful work for women with barriers to employment. But no. I wanted to be a real, for-profit business. I wanted to run alongside every other corporation out there to show them that a business can make money and do good.

Businesses that give back—or social enterprises—were few and far between when I started the Etsy shop in 2009. At that point, there was only one that I knew of—a shoe company had recently launched the new concept of using a profitable business to make a difference. Buy a pair of shoes, and they would give a pair of shoes to a child in South Africa, Argentina,

Ethiopia, or even children in America who needed them. People felt good about spending their money with TOMS and wearing their shoes that did good.

While I didn't know it at the time, some other grassroots businesses were starting up alongside mine. We all were working away in our closets and spare bedrooms and rented studio spaces to grow businesses that had purpose and meaning while also offering a great product. Some of them were designing jewelry and wondering how they could make their products have purpose bigger than being just a beautiful necklace or beaded earrings. Some of them were wanting to create jobs for women in various countries and wondering what product they could create that would bridge the need for jobs with the pocketbooks of American women. The goal wasn't to make a lot of money. And the goal wasn't to ask for donations. The goal was to find a product that could support a mission that made our hearts beat faster and gave purpose to the product—not only for the person making it but for the consumer as well.

God was doing something here with business as a mission, and I was excited for Better Life Bags to become another for-profit business that also did good. But I wasn't sure how our customers would react to this new idea. Our prices were much higher than many other bag companies out there. We were hiring women in America and paying them well for their work—and doing that wasn't cheap. Would customers understand that? And would they want to join us in our mission to give meaningful work to these women by purchasing our bags—even at their current price points?

I had no choice but to keep walking forward to find out.

|||||||||||||||||||||||||||||||||||||||||||||||||||||||||||||||||||||||||||||

In 2014 I was invited to speak to a group of women who belonged to a country club in Indiana. Many of them were married to CEOs of companies and other influencers of their communities. I wasn't sure these women were my target market, but I agreed to go and speak to them. I was honored to be asked and grateful for the chance to share the story of what God was building at Better Life Bags.

This was my first speaking engagement, and I wanted to do the story justice. I sat down to write out my speech, and the words came quick and fast. The story was so fun to write down—how the Etsy shop had started, how I'd hired Nadia, how I'd seen the impact each job was having on the women in my community and in me. It was as if I were a reporter, coming in from the outside and writing the story of what I had seen. It was the first time I had intentionally looked back at all the special stickers I'd collected along the way that had led me to this point.

I knew the country club women would be familiar with investments and return on investments from their financial accounts—both personal and business. So I decided to get gutsy at the end of my speech. Gripping the podium and crossing my toes that I wouldn't get booed off the stage, I said, "As a business, I don't feel that we are doing anything extra special. I believe all businesses should be investing in their employees the way we do. Of course we are thinking about profits and growth because to be able to help anyone, we need to remain financially sustainable. But looking out for the good of each individual? And acknowledging the God-given dignity that they already have? I'm out to prove to corporate America that you can think about more than the bottom line when it comes to structuring your business."

There was no booing yet, so I held the podium a little

tighter and continued, "There is no greater return on invest-ment than when you invest in people. In their futures. In their families. And in their souls. We want to see profits, but we also want people to feel loved. We want to grow our company, but we also want to see people's hearts and lives changed. In the end of this life, only a few things will remain. Our positions, our money, our titles, and our companies will be gone. But the souls of people will remain. We want to invest in that."

I looked up from my notes to women crying, wiping their eyes with their napkins. There was a brief moment of silence that felt like hours, and then a standing ovation with lots of clapping.

America was ready for this type of business! People's hearts were ripe and open to considering the impact our pur-chases were having on those who were making our products. They didn't care about only the quality of the final product; they wanted the quality of the life of the person who made it to be better too. It was the beginning of something big. I could feel it.

Today it's almost impossible to find a company that doesn't give back in some way. In ten short years, our business—along with the amazing purchasing power of our customers—has joined other businesses in helping turn the tide of what is acceptable business practice in America and around the world.

It's not enough anymore to just give one dollar of every sale to a random charity. Customers want real change and real good to be done with their money in exchange for a high-quality product.

I couldn't be prouder to have been a tiny part of that change.

The world was ready for a missional business, but was Better Life Bags ready for the world? I knew that customers expected high-quality products. Our bags weren't mass-produced by factory machines. They were handmade on sewing machines by skilled seamstresses in our community. And because of this, it meant that not every seam was a perfect quarter inch from the edge. It meant that sometimes the label was sewn slightly off center. It meant that a bag would come back with a small pen mark on the leather or a tiny cut in the fabric lining. Our hearts would sink each time we found a small error in an otherwise perfect bag. We would carry the flawed bag around in our arms like a sick child and ask other people to examine the flaw. Could we send the bag anyway? Even with the tiny pen mark that the customer might not ever notice? It was so tempting sometimes. To remake the bag would mean rushing it through the entire process and emailing the customer to let them know their bag would be a few days late. It also meant a loss of revenue. We would end up with a bag that we couldn't sell at full price. These flawed bags would pile up over time until we had a large enough collection to host a warehouse sale in the summer to sell them at a serious discount. So all was not lost, but man, it really hurt whenever we would find one of those mess-ups.

Our eyes would fill with compassion as we would look at the person carrying the sad bag—wordlessly agreeing that we couldn't send out a less-than-perfect product. I knew one thing deep down in my heart. If we were going to be a missional business and show the world that a for-profit company could do good with its resources, we needed to have an exceptional product.

I never wanted someone to receive one of our bags in the mail, be disappointed in its quality, and say, "Oh, well, it was for a good cause." I wanted our bags to be desirable in and of themselves—regardless of our missional focus. I wanted the mission of hiring women from our community to be the cherry on top, the added bonus to an already amazing bag.

But this didn't come naturally. It meant a lot of training for our seamstresses, who cared deeply about doing a quality job and meeting expectations. It meant that we created standards that every seamstress had to abide by—sewing with identical quarter-inch seams, using a template to center the label, and putting the zipper in the bag the same way as everyone else. We moved from trying to make as many bags as we could to keep up with the demand to making those bags as best as we could to keep the demand coming. It also meant that we researched and experimented with new ways to make our bags so they transitioned from a product that looked handmade to one that could compete with other bags on the national market. We figured out how to roll our straps in thirds so the raw edge of the leather was hidden instead of exposed. We discovered a way to hide the stitching on our magnets so they became a seamless, almost invisible, part of the design. When we received feedback that a few of our metal clasps were breaking after a few months of use, we found new clasps that were much higher quality—but also four times the price. With only a tiny bit of hesitation, I decided to switch to the higher quality, more expensive clasps. Having a product that I could stand behind and was proud of was more important than the cost.

I was developing a mission to create a high-quality product that provided high-quality jobs for women in our community. Every decision was filtered through this. If we considered adding or retiring a bag style, I would ask myself whether doing so would take work away from a seamstress who wanted it. I would see whether we could price the product reasonably. And I would make sure that what we were designing was done in a way that maintained our high quality standards.

Assigning a mission—knowing why you are doing something—is crucial to your success. It gives you something to work toward and a purpose for your days.

When you assign a mission to your mothering—to raise children who are kind, creative, and compassionate—your days are assigned meaning. Your hours become purposeful. You no longer get upset about a cup of spilled milk because your mission isn't to raise children who don't have accidents. You don't discipline over a broken toy, but you do over harsh words spewed toward a sibling, because you want to emphasize that relationships are more important than things. You commit to attending church every Sunday even if it means missing the semifinal tee-ball game because you've decided that putting God first is a value for your family. Or you decide to skip church and attend the tee-ball game because you want to show that God is not rigid in his rules and as much worship can happen on a ball field as it can in a church pew. You focus on the behaviors that do or don't result in the culture of kindness and compassion you want to cultivate.

When you assign a mission to your marriage—to put someone else's needs above your own—you wake up every day with an assignment to love your spouse the way you want to be loved. It doesn't feel like a sacrifice or burden to make breakfast or fold his clothes because you've been assigned a mission to accomplish. You secretly fill up his car with gas on the way home from running errands because you hate it when you get into the car at the beginning of a full day and realize you have an empty gas tank. You tidy up the house thirty minutes before he arrives home—not because you're a housewife from 1950 but because you love to walk into a tidy home after a long day and assume he will too. As you spend more years together, you learn the specific quirks and details he appreciates about life. You make it your mission to surprise and delight him with those things, such as ordering your husband those American flag running shorts he keeps talking about even though you think they might look ridiculous, or going ahead and loading the dishwasher using the method he prefers because it bothers him more than it inconveniences you. The mission to love your husband the way you want to be loved drives the actions and gives meaning to your actions. Hopefully, he has the same mission to love and serve you in this way, and the result is two people who are filled up and able to turn around and pour their gifts and energies back into the world.

Interestingly, not many people assign a mission to what they do. Not many people take the time to think through why they do what they do. In his book Start with Why, Simon Sinek says, "Very few people or companies can clearly articulate WHY they do WHAT they do.... By WHY I mean what is your purpose, cause or belief? WHY does your company exist? WHY do you get out of bed every morning? And WHY should anyone care?"[1]

Everything with a mission attached becomes bigger than we are. It's not the cherry on top—it's the foundation of anything worthwhile. If you're struggling with an area in your life, assign a mission to it. Why are you in school? Why did you apply for that particular job? Why are you repainting your house? Why are you buying that bag?

---

1   Simon Sinek, *Start with Why: How Great Leaders Inspire Everyone to Take Action* (New York: Portfolio, 2009), 39.

Our customers at Better Life Bags have a mission in purchasing. They have defined a mission for their money—to only use their dollars to help make the world a better place. When it comes time for them to buy a new bag or shirt or pair of shoes, they funnel their choices through their mission until a handful of companies shake out at the bottom. These people—our customers (you!)—have become some of my favorite people to hang out with on the internet. Our community has rallied around one another—specifically in the VIP Facebook group—not only because we all love bags but because we love the mission to create meaningful work. And we know there can't be any meaningful work without bag orders.

The custom aspect of our bags is something that draws the customer even deeper into the mission of our company and gives them a tangible way to connect and feel a part of our bigger mission. Our customers are designing and building their own bags on our website. It's been like this from the beginning. Customers have always been able to pick out their fabric for each area of the bag—even before we added the leather option.

At first, to make this happen, I would get a sense from the customer about what colors and patterns she liked, and I would trot off to the fabric store to take pictures of everything I saw that might be a possibility. This, mind you, was in the age before smartphones. Nowadays, I could video chat with customers in the fabric aisles. Or at the very least have a texting conversation complete with pictures and immediate feedback on their likes and dislikes.

But back in 2009, I would take my small Sony camera to the fabric store, shoot pictures of tons of fabrics, come home, take out the small SD card, plug that into my computer, and finally email the options to the customer. When the customer chose their favorites, I would run back to the fabric store with my fingers crossed that those particular prints would still be in stock. It was a time-consuming and tedious process.

To make the fabric selection process easier, I decided to open a wholesale account with a fabric supplier about a year later. The problem was that opening a wholesale account with a fabric supplier would mean an opening order of $1,500. I hadn't even sold five hundred dollars' worth of bags yet. Neil and I talked it over and decided this might be the next step for Better Life Bags. While it would limit the fabric choices to only what I had in stock, it would give me back the hours of time I spent taking pictures, driving to and from the fabric store, and emailing with customers. This way I could have bolts of fabric in my own living room, ready to be cut into bags. I ordered a collection of fun prints and marveled at all the extra time I had to sew bags instead of running around.

The custom aspect of our bag-making business set us apart as Etsy grew. The popularity of that website grew exponentially, and as customers beyond my friends and family visited our Etsy shop, I was starting to find the custom process cumbersome since there was not a way for the customer's fabric options to come through directly on their order form. In early 2013 we decided to take another leap and hired a web developer to create a website for us. We left the safety net of Etsy and ventured off into the internet on our own. With this new website, we also built custom software to make the bag customization process fun, interactive, and easy. Customers could click on various thumbnail pictures of fabric options and see their choices pop up on a virtual bag. They could essentially build their own bag and see it come together right before their eyes.

This website wasn't cheap. As with the buy-in for the

wholesale fabric account four years earlier, it felt risky to spend so much on a website. But our mission was to create jobs, and I knew if our website were easier to navigate and our bags were simpler to customize, more customers would buy bags—and more women could be given meaningful work.

Little did I know that women would literally spend hours playing on this new website. It was so fun to see how the bag changed with the various fabric and leather colors being switched around. My husband lovingly calls it "a video game for women." And he is right.

But the best part was that this interactive website was essentially inviting our customers closer into the mission. A customer knew that after she had the fun experience of designing and purchasing her own bag, the fabric would be cut by Jubilee, and the leather would be cut by Sabah. The pieces would be collated and collected and organized into piles by Elise and piled into a plastic bin for Umme to take home. Umme would pick up her box on Wednesday, pull out the pieces of leather and fabric, and sew them together in such a way as to replicate the exact design the customer had created on the website. When Umme returned her finished bags the next week, the straps would be sewn on by Jennifer, then set in the shipping bin for Lizzie to burn the loose threads and double-check that the exact design the customer selected is what she would hold in her hands. Lizzie would also package the bag up in homemade dustbags made by Roushanara and Shaheda and then set them in the box to wait for a label. The label would be printed, and the post office would pick up the box, starting the bag on its final journey to the customer.

Without the purposeful purchase of a Better Life Bag, our women would not have work to do. Our customer doesn't have to start a company of her own to do good in this world. She doesn't have to volunteer or donate money. No matter where she lives, she can join in our mission of providing meaningful work for women who have barriers to traditional employment, and she receives a high-quality custom bag in return. Her purchase has purpose. Her dollars have been given an important task.

Everything works better when there's a mission behind it. Spending money feels better when we know exactly how our money is being used to make a difference in the world. Going to work is tolerable when we know the reason why we are there. You can endure waking up early to work on a side business only when the purpose behind it is something you deeply believe in.

The mission cannot be a by-product of the work. The mission is the heartbeat of the work.

CHAPTER 5

Tear Down the Fence

Welcome to My Little Country
House in the City

|||||||||||||||||||||||||||||||||||||||||||||||||||||||||||||||||||||||

While God was busy answering a big prayer of mine with Better Life Bags, I never imagined he would also answer my prayer for a house in Hamtramck with a big backyard for my ever-growing gaggle of children to play in. We were pregnant with baby number three and needed to move out of our small apartment home and finally buy a house. My requirements for a house were still stairs to the second level inside and a big backyard. That was it.

We house-shopped for almost a year, which basically consisted of walking into house after house and immediately turning around. Most were so dirty and stained with mold that the thought of renovating was too overwhelming. One house gave me vertigo as we walked through, the floors actually tilting like a carnival ride. Another house had a shower in the middle of the floor plan—with a window that looked into the living room. I guess this allowed you to watch TV while washing your hair? Most homes had two kitchens since they were originally designed to be duplexes—one apartment on the first floor and the other on the second. While this wasn't a deal breaker, buying a home with two kitchens when we planned to use the home for one family seemed a bit excessive, and I knew I would want to tear the upstairs kitchen out as soon as we could. What a mess and huge undertaking.

After searching for so long, the prayer for a normal single-family home seemed too impossible. Until one day we walked up five cement stairs and opened the door into a carpeted two-story house. The carpet—stained with dog pee—could be removed, I told myself as I stepped inside. I turned to the left and was met with the stairs to the second level. Stairs inside the house! This meant the house wasn't a duplex and would likely have only one kitchen.

I made my way through the bottom level and walked into a kitchen straight from 1970. We pulled up a corner of the linoleum and found original hardwood. The brown beadboard that wrapped around the entire bottom half of the kitchen could be painted white, and the dated cabinet doors could be switched out to tide me over until we could completely redo the kitchen. When I opened the back door and was met with an extra-long yard, I was sold. I hadn't even seen the upstairs yet—which, by the way, wasn't finished out; it was just studs, so no kitchen up there. But I knew as soon as I saw the yard that this was our home. I could imagine my kids having space to run through all that grass. A newly planted tree held so much potential for tree climbing as it grew bigger and stronger. And the detached garage had an automatic door opener. These were the little luxuries that were hard to come by in our city. I

felt so seen by God. Even with an entire upstairs in shambles—
the previous owners abandoned a renovation—I could see that
this home answered so many of my prayers. Like a father picking out the best for his child, I knew God had saved this house
in Hamtramck for me.

We had three months to finish off the upstairs so that we
could have bedrooms to sleep in before the baby came. Our
new neighbor ended up being a general contractor, and he
came to teach my husband and me how to cut out long planks
of urine-stained hardwood floorboards and replace them with
new pieces. I bought kneepads and spent month seven of my
pregnancy using a handheld round saw to pull out all the
planks we wanted to replace before someone came to sand
and refinish all that hardwood that had been hiding under the
carpet. Other friends stepped into paper-thin paint suits and
took to the ceilings and closets with white paint. Everything
was painted white or light gray. I was new to owning my own
home and afraid of making design decisions that I would later
regret. Plus, by the time I was thirty-eight weeks pregnant, I
was hoping every wall would have a fresh coat applied and the
crib would have somewhere to land before Corbin Patrick was
scheduled to arrive on December 30.

The family next door to us had two kids similar in age to
my oldest two children. Jonah and Isabel—their oldest—ended
up in the same preschool class that year. As most kids do, they
quickly became fast friends, looking past any differences and
simply seeing a fun playmate to run and bike and draw with.
We would lift them high over the chain-link fence between
our yards so they could play with one another. They went back
and forth between yards—sometimes as frequently as every
hour—and came inside only for bathroom and snack breaks.

These neighbors had moved to Hamtramck for reasons

similar to ours—to invest in this diverse community and use their urban farming expertise to increase economic growth for the city. They were an American family who had returned to Chicago from living in Yemen a few years prior and longed to be back surrounded by Yemeni food, people, and culture. Hamtramck was a perfect location for them because of the large Yemeni population here. They saw a need for fresh produce in the city and recognized that Detroit and Hamtramck had a lot of overgrown and abandoned lots that could be turned into farmland. Not only could they sell the produce at local farmers markets, but the farm itself could be a job creation program for local men and women in Hamtramck. It resonated so much with Better Life Bags and our mission to hire women from our community. We had an immediate connection with this family, and it was providence that within the span of a few months, we both bought homes that sat next door to each other, with only a chain-link fence separating our properties.

We eventually cut that fence down. Our two families were becoming more than just neighbors. We were teammates, both here to create jobs and relationships in Hamtramck. We shared everything—lawn mowers, cars, eggs, sugar, and even traded babysitting hours for weekly date nights. On cool nights, we would all sit around a spontaneous campfire in our firepit and roast marshmallows while the kids ran and wrestled in the grass. It felt like living next door to family. Cutting down the fence seemed as if it were a metaphorical picture of tearing down any barriers to this communal way of living. I remember the day Neil walked out with large wire cutters and went to town on that chain-link fence. Our kids were so excited to be able to run freely between the yards. It wasn't long before Fatima, the Bangladeshi neighbor girl two houses down, started coming over regularly to play with the kids, especially after we bought a swing set and set it up between the two yards that were now connected.

The empty house that sat on the other side of us had been a mother-in-law house to ours, so it never had a fence, and it had remained empty since we bought our house. The kids took free rein of that yard as well—until the "For Sale" sign came down. We cautiously awaited the first glimpse of our new neighbors. We desperately hoped the buyers would also have kids so our backyard "park" could continue to expand.

"A girl! They have a girl!" my daughter exclaimed as we watched the moving truck unload.

They sure did. Another family from Bangladesh had arrived with a daughter around the same age as the other kids in the backyard kids' club. Boy, was she in for a treat—I hoped. We invited her over to play on our swing set, and she timidly came. That timid nature started shedding a few days later as we heard fits of giggles and screams of delight coming from our backyard playground. That summer, all the neighbor kids were drawn to each other like magnets, and all four houses in a row had gathered some sort of play equipment to keep the children outside and entertained. One home had rescued a free kids' playhouse from Facebook Marketplace that everyone loved to climb on. Our yard became headquarters for s'more-making and swing-set-playing. The next yard was wide open grass for soccer and baseball. And the favorite addition to the backyard row was when Fatima's family bought a trampoline.

One day Neil and I were relaxing in front of our firepit, watching kids jump and swing and kick balls back and forth to each other. He made a startling comment to me.

"Becky, where else would you find a swing set, a trampoline, a playhouse, and still lots of grass to play around in?"

"In the *country*, babe," I replied without hesitation as my heart sometimes dreamed of a quieter life with even more space to run and play. I was trying to show Neil that we could have this exact setup at our own quaint farmhouse in the country. But in his wisdom and ability to see a different side to everything, he replied, "Yeah, but you wouldn't have the constant playmates of these neighbor kids whenever you stepped foot outside."

He was right. This was a blessing. My heart sometimes yearned for country living after so many years in the city, but what we had right here seemed to be the best of both worlds. God was creating a community of friends with the expanse of combined backyards to give me my little country house in the city. This house was a gift—another special sticker that God had dropped along my path. It was the perfect home for us.

Two summers later, I was pulling weeds out of our ever-expanding garden and looked up to see Fatima's dad outside with his wire cutters. He was cutting a gate in the chain-link fence between their yard and our neighbor's. As the backyard park continued to expand, more and more fences were being torn down to ease the access to each other's lives.

||||||||||||||||||||||||||||||||||||||||||||||||||||||||||||||||||||||||

Ironically, while our neighborhood block was cutting down fences between yards, our country was putting up walls and closing down borders.

I didn't realize this fully at the time, but God moving us to Hamtramck—a city of many immigrants and Muslims—was not an accident. This became obvious to me on the tenth anniversary of 9/11. The news tributes and Facebook posts took me right back to that morning on September 11, 2001, when

Muslim extremists flew airplanes into the sides of the World Trade Center. As a freshman in college, I stood transfixed by the small television in our dorm room—one tower burning as we all tried to figure out what had just happened. An airplane must have accidentally hit the tower in New York City, I thought, trying to explain and understand what I was watching. But as I watched a second airplane hit the second tower, I knew it wasn't an accident. Someone was attacking America, and everyone across the country was watching it live.

In 2001 I didn't know much about Muslim culture, and there weren't any Muslim people living in my small town in Illinois that I knew of. Of course, I knew other religions and cultures existed around the world, but this was my first introduction to terrorism and suicide missions. Suddenly, everyone was talking about how terrible it was that Muslim people were willing to kill people—and themselves—in the name of Allah (or God). How twisted their view of God must be to think he would ask this of them. I felt sad for them and scared of them all at once.

Perhaps it was because everyone was in shock, but none of the news outlets did a great job that day of explaining the difference between Muslim people and Islamic terrorists. We all grew up that morning, realizing that our America might not be as safe as we once thought. And the enemy must be Muslim people.

Shortly after 9/11, I had an airplane flight scheduled. I remember walking into Chicago O'Hare International Airport and seeing a Muslim man waiting at the same gate as I was. He was dressed in a white button-down shirt and white cotton pants and sandals. He had a turban on his head. My heart stopped. Was this man about to hijack my airplane? Was I safe? I looked around to see whether any other passengers seemed worried or alarmed. A few were giving him the side-eye—trying not to appear as though they were staring—while hiding their faces behind newspapers or magazines.

Of course, the flight took off and landed without issue, and I started to understand that not every Muslim man is interested in blowing up America. Not every Muslim is a terrorist. After moving to Hamtramck and meeting Muslim men and women in the flesh, I learned that most Muslim people denounce the actions of these Islamic extremists. Most Muslim people are trying to raise kids and make a living and take care of their yards. Most Muslim people tell funny jokes and cry at sad movies and enjoy listening to music. Most Muslim people in the United States want to be upstanding Americans and love this country. Most Muslim people are just like me. There was nothing scary about them.

But on the tenth anniversary of September 11, I realized that many Americans were still afraid of Muslims. I heard news reports and watched people protest the rising popula-tion of Muslims in the neighboring city of Đearborn. They didn't want another mosque built. They wanted Muslims to "go home to their country," even though many of them are American-born citizens. They came all the way from Florida to hold signs and recite the Pledge of Allegiance in front of Dearborn's largest mosque, afraid of "world domination." I looked at the Muslim seamstresses we had hired at Better Life Bags—women I had hugged and eaten lunch with and received gifts from—and tried to imagine how devastating it was to feel as if you weren't welcome in the country you lived in. I pictured their husbands and their sons and their brothers being lumped into the category of terrorist, and it all made me sad that the unthinkable actions of a few had altered the way an entire group of people were treated and viewed.

In 2015 Hamtramck elected the first Muslim-majority city council in the US, and reporters from all around the world flocked here to interview business owners and residents. They all wanted to know whether we were scared. Our "melting pot" of a city was fascinating to outsiders. How could so many cultures and languages and people be crammed into two square miles and not be constantly in conflict with one another?

We aren't a perfect community, of course. There is sometimes a blanket of fear that falls over the city—especially around election season. But on a normal Tuesday, we are just friendly neighbors waving to each other as we leave in the morning and making small talk as we get our mail.

When our new president closed the borders to our country in 2017, hysteria seemed to be at an all-time high. America was too afraid of who was already here and who might be coming in, so we closed the borders. We instituted a "Muslim ban." And the crazy prayer that Nadia and I had begged God for—that the rest of her family would be able to come here from Yemen—seemed to do more than fade away. It felt truly impossible now.

When I arrived at Nadia's house that week to talk about how she was feeling, she was crying. She was fearful that she would never be hugged by her mother or see her little brothers again. As an American, I was frustrated. I wanted to apologize for the president's actions, telling her that this was not the America that I knew and believed in and wanted to be a part of. This was not my America. She knew it wasn't my fault, but we still sat on her couch and mourned any progress that had been made in getting her family to the States. At the end, I reminded her that God was bigger than any of these rules, and that if he wanted to, her family would still be given a miraculous green light to come.

I remember watching my Facebook feed the week our borders closed, as the protests, blog posts, news articles, and hysteria flooded in. CNN flashed a graphic to help us visualize all the countries that were no longer invited in. These countries were marked in red. My neighbors' native countries were red. My seamstresses' native countries were red. The teachers and aides at my son's school came from countries that were marked in red. These were my friends. And their families. I was confused. And I had questions. Lots of them.

Who said we could close the borders? How had these countries been chosen? What about the refugees? What about the card holders? And how did the vetting process work? Was the president right to do this? Or was he just plain wrong? Should I stand up to him? How do I stand up for my neighbors? What about faith? What about Jesus? What was my role? What part did I play?

It all became too much, like standing on the wrong side of a batting cage—dodging fastballs as more and more information and persuasion and hype came flying at me on my computer screen. So many people were trying to tell me which side was right and which side was wrong and where I needed to stand on the issue as a God-fearing, Jesus-loving girl.

I found myself swirling because I was so easily swayed to any side. I could understand the fear because sometimes I felt it too. I could understand wanting to interview and conduct a background check on every person entering America to ensure the safety of our citizens. And I could understand wanting to reduce the number of people moving to our already crowded cities. But to shut the borders down and lock the gate without taking each individual situation into account seemed drastic and harsh.

I decided to take a walk to clear my head. I passed

protestors at city hall—right outside the building where our Muslim-majority city council met on a regular basis. They were holding signs that read "Refugees Are Welcome Here," "My Grandparents Were Refugees," "We Stand with Our Muslim Neighbors," and "Don't Send Me Back." Little girls in hijabs waved American flags. Black Americans held hands with Arab women. White women linked arms with black women. Hamtramck was standing strong and protecting each other. One protester carried an upside-down American flag—a sign of distress. I wondered whether I should have been standing in the middle of that crowd too. And if so, what would I have written on my sign?

"What if your life were a daily protest, Rebecca?" I heard that whisper deep within my soul as I kept walking. It was a special sticker encouraging me to keep working that thought out, telling me it was important. Standing and protesting on a Saturday morning in the city square was important and effective, but what I did and how I acted on a Monday evening in my own backyard next to my Muslim neighbors was what mattered. America could be closing its borders, but I could still reach out my hand.

I passed a group of Arab high school students returning from a visit to the local library. They were carrying "I LOVE the Library" plastic sacks. Their American teacher walked on the part of the sidewalk closest to the road—a sign of protection, I noticed.

One oblivious teenage girl crouched down right in my path, forcing me to stop. I stood awkwardly, watching her scoop up snow with her bare hands that reached out from behind the black fabric she wore. Maybe it was one of the first times she'd experienced the cold whiteness. Her eyes caught mine as she stood up, and I smiled. I couldn't see any part of her face except her eyes, but I knew she was smiling back. Eyes tell so much about a person.

I hoped my smile could convey everything my confused heart was feeling. I wanted this simple bit of eye contact to cross language barriers and break down walls. I wanted to tell her she was welcome here with me. To tell her I was glad she had come.

While Facebook was loud and jarring that weekend, the actual streets of my city felt contrastingly quiet—contemplative and wounded, confused and hurting, but not angry.

Life as a daily protest. The thought came again.

I didn't need to be in the crowd holding signs, I decided. Instead, I need to be in living rooms, embraced in hugs, sharing meals with my immigrant neighbors. Life as a daily protest didn't have a day, time, and place attached to a flyer or Facebook event. This type of protest could happen daily, and at any time, here in my city. It could happen through the generous smiles, curious questions, cross-culture friendships, and genuine neighborly way of living. When a president closes our borders, we can open our front doors. When a news station tells us we should be scared, we can pursue friendship and find common interests. And when signs tell our neighbors to go home, we can whisper that they already are.

Wars are not always won through protests or on battle-fields or in courts or by way of Facebook posts. They are won in relationships. On couches. Through the sharing of friend-ship, tears, and laughter. They are won by rising above the stereotypes and getting to know the person beneath.

I guess it's fine for someone to go to the protest, to hold the sign, to carry the upside-down American flag. The kingdom of God is pretty upside down in its thinking, after all. But don't go home afterward and be done. Don't turn on your computer and start posting the articles and fighting a Facebook battle as your only contribution.

I remember reading an angry post from a Facebook friend telling me—and everyone else reading—that if I didn't speak up and take a side on social media with a comment or post, it was the same as choosing the side of the oppressor.

I disagree.

I decided to protest differently. I decided that day that my movements would be small and quiet, not blasted publicly all over social media. I didn't have to share three blog posts and a news article on my Facebook wall to choose a side. For me, the better way was to enter into a relationship with the affected party. To become friends with someone different from myself. To boldly step out over my cultural comfort line and enter a neighbor's world.

I remember the first day I hired an African American woman, Casandra, to come work at Better Life Bags. She walked in, and the room became quiet. The women from Bangladesh who were sewing together around the table literally stopped talking immediately. I figured it must be because someone new had walked in.

I got Casandra set up at a leather-cutting station and showed her a few pieces to start cutting. And then I let her be and sat back down at my computer to answer customer emails. One of my seamstresses crept up to me so quietly that I jumped when she whispered in my ear, "I'm really scared."

"Scared of what?" I whispered back.

Her eyes moved toward Casandra, and suddenly it all made sense. This was probably the first time these women had ever been in such close quarters with an African American. And the only thing they knew about a person with this color of skin was what they had seen in the movies (but that's a whole separate conversation about how terribly wrong that is) or what their friends and family had told them (which is another entire conversation about how powerful our words to our children are). In these women's minds, African Americans were to be feared. They were dangerous. And they needed to be careful when they saw one.

My mind and heart instantly went back to my first few weeks in Hamtramck, when everything was different and scary and I swore I would never be friends with any of my neighbors. Somehow in the process of finding my place in Hamtramck, a little handbag business had crept slowly into the cracks of my life, filling up any extra time I had and spilling over into my life so much that I had to reach out for help. And whom did I reach out to? A stranger who had nothing in common with me. Or so I thought.

Those weekly visits to Nadia's laid a foundation. The walks to the park with our kids while we talked about our big God-dreams and shared the prayers of our hearts—they were setting a framework. The nights when we would call each other crying after a fight with our husbands or a hard day with our kids, or the times I would go over to her house, bringing along worship music about God's closeness in the hard times—they were the final nails being hammered into this thing being built.

Nadia and I had become friends.

Somehow.

Somewhere along the way, the uncomfortable melted away and left the foundation of what we both had in common. We were both mothers. We both loved to sew. We both had dreams and hopes and fears. We both had stepped beyond the boundaries and comfort of our cultures and entered each other's lives with open hands and trembling hearts. We had cut down the fence between us, snipping metal chain links one by one until the entire structure collapsed and we were able to travel back and forth freely between our two lives.

I knew exactly how my seamstresses were feeling when Casandra walked in for her first day of work because I had been there. But standing years down the road with a stranger-turned-friend by my side, I knew they would get there too. Their daily interactions with each other started with a simple hello and a smile, then moved to conversations about their weekends and plans for the holiday. They cooked for each other and discovered new favorite foods together. They joined together in this mission to make high-quality custom bags. And now my seamstresses and Casandra hug every day before they leave, calling each other friend and wishing each other a good night. What an unexpected outcome of what began as a tiny little purse shop!

I'm sure you've also found yourself in situations where your instincts have screamed at you to run, not because it was dangerous but because it was uncomfortable. Like my seamstresses, you were also scared. You walked into that new Bible study and realized you were the only person who looked like you, and you weren't sure whether you were welcome. You started a new job and realized you were the least experienced person working there. Or you started volunteering for the PTO and wondered whether you had what it took to even stand next to those superhero moms with the picturesque children who always had their hair brushed.

Situations such as these can make me clam up. It's very tempting to close the door to my heart and cross my arms over my chest for protection. I try to convince myself that if I am left alone, my heart can't be hurt. No one can tell me I don't fit in because I'm not even allowing myself the chance to find a fit. No one can make me feel unwanted because I'm not even allowing myself to want to be there. I put up my fences and boundaries and stay hidden behind them. Safe. Or so I think.

But what if I—and all of us—assumed a posture of arms open wide? What if when we found ourselves as part of the majority, we verbally reached out and extended a welcome to the minority? What if when we found ourselves as part of the minority, we courageously took steps toward the uncomfortable and put on a brave smile?

What if by cutting down the fences, you find your new best friend? What if by cutting down the fences, you discover a new career path? What if by cutting down the fences, you make enough space to let others in too?

Maybe by cutting down the fences, you too will end up with the yard of your dreams.

CHAPTER 6

Let the Dream Simmer

Let's Talk about Fly Balls and Betta Fish

||||||||||||||||||||||||||||||||||||||||||||||||||||||||||||||||||||||||||||||

As Better Life Bags has grown and attracted more eyes and a larger audience, women have emailed to ask me how they can grow something the same way I did. I've jumped on phone calls to listen to dreams about starting clothing companies. I've sat next to visitors who have come for a tour of Better Life Bags and shared their ideas for making soap. And I've waded through my social media direct messages as women shared their hearts about wanting to reach out to their neighbors or welcome refugees into their homes. After listening to handfuls of business ideas and book concepts and ministry ventures, I've realized that most of them can be placed into two categories of dreams: fly balls, the kind that drop into your lap, and betta fish, the ones you're afraid to invest in because they might die.

I've experienced both types in my life. Better Life Bags was the fly ball. This book was the fish.

Let me explain.

Better Life Bags and the company it is today came as a complete surprise. I wasn't looking into or trying to build a business. This dream was hit to me like a fly ball. I was standing in the outfield of life—picking flowers, watching clouds—and heard someone yell, "You! You! You! It's coming for you!" I snapped to attention, held my glove in the air, and caught the dream coming my way. It was a ball in motion from the moment I started, and I just kept running after it to see where it led. This is not to say these dreams are easy or quick avenues to success—later in the book you'll read more about the incredible challenges and hard seasons I've walked through because of Better Life Bags. These fly-ball-type dreams are hit our way when we aren't expecting them, and because we chose to reach up and catch them instead of cowering and running, we are sent off on an adventure.

A lot of life is determined by fly balls. A dog shows up on your front porch and doesn't leave. No one claims him despite hanging "Lost Dog" flyers everywhere, so you invite him in and adopt that sweet little guy. Or maybe you go out for a fun girls' night with friends—and end up meeting a guy instead. One date turns into four, and you have a ring on your finger before the end of the year. Maybe a relative suddenly dies and leaves you their home in the mountains, so you decide to pick up everything and move there for a new start. These are the dreams and pathways that are surprises to us—ones we couldn't have dreamed about because we didn't know they could exist. Once they become ours, though—we have to work to keep them alive.

But I think more often than not, dreams are more like pet store fish—we aren't really sure how long they'll last.

One day, shortly after we bought our new house with the

massive backyard, we found ourselves out shopping for a toilet. This house had only one bathroom, and the toilet didn't work. I had dreamed about remodeling the kitchen or installing a gas fireplace in the living room, but our first—and most practical—purchase needed to be a working toilet.

The hardware store where we bought the toilet was right next to the pet shop. As we walked out carrying our new porcelain throne, our kids begged us to go look at the fish. Pet stores are basically free zoos, so after we loaded our toilet into the trunk, we obliged. I should have seen this coming, but we didn't walk out of that pet store empty-handed. Apparently, our children had their own dream—owning a fish—and the only thing standing in the way of making that dream a reality was the checkout line and our wallets. So we picked out the two most beautiful betta fish, named them Blue and Red, and carried them home.

It wasn't until we hit a few potholes in the road, the car jolted, and I struggled to balance two plastic tubs of fish on my lap that I remembered the toilet in the trunk. Wouldn't you know? We had bought the fish and the fish's graveyard on the same shopping trip. The dream and the death. It was only a matter of time before the two would meet.

I think a lot of times we do this with our dreams after they are birthed in our hearts—buy a toilet to flush them before they get a chance to live. You get an idea for something you might like to do with your life, but before you can even make an action plan, you kill that dream with fears, doubts, or insecurities. Maybe you decide that it looks fun to join your friend's multilevel marketing team to make a little extra money on the side, but before you can even ask your friend questions, fear creeps in and tells you that you aren't a salesperson and you don't want to be that one friend on Facebook that annoys everyone with their offers. Maybe you want to lose some weight, but before you can research plans or go grocery shopping for fruits and vegetables, doubt creeps up and whispers in your ear that you have always been a little fluffy and nothing is going to change. Maybe you want to start a business, but you're overwhelmed with where to start and decide it's just too hard and you don't have what it takes.

I know some of our dreams seem big and unattainable—scary and out of reach. I felt this way too. Ever since I was in elementary school, I've wanted to write a book. I turned in a typewriter-produced, hand-illustrated submission to the Young Authors Writing Contest every year. I never won. When I entered high school, I quit trying to win the competition and started writing for myself in journal after journal—now stored in a watertight bin in my basement. College brought computers and Word documents, and I continued writing. And when Better Life Bags was a tiny little baby shop, I started a Better Life blog along with it as a place to keep writing and documenting the journey.

That dream to write a book never went away. I didn't flush that dream down the toilet just because I wasn't sure how to pursue a writing career. I simply enjoyed writing in the ways I knew how by blogging and journaling. I even tried my hand at writing poems and music in college. My ears perked up whenever I heard someone mention they were writing a book. I took note of publishing company names on the spines of books that I read. I started following authors on social media and cheered on my online friends as they got book deals. All the while, I wondered whether it might ever be my turn, but I never said that out loud until the night of our eighth wedding anniversary.

Neil and I snagged an Uber Black, an upscale ride, for the first time and had reservations at a fancy restaurant in downtown Detroit. We started talking about things we would like to do in our lifetimes. Dreams. Goals. Wishes. With Better Life Bags growing so quickly, I needed to think and dream bigger. What else would I like to do with my one wild and precious life?

"What do you want to do now that you've successfully grown a business? What's your next dream?" he asked.

"I think I'd like to write a book," I said after thinking for a long while and mustering up the courage to finally speak out loud the dream I'd held inside for so long. But there was a heavy emphasis on that simple little five-letter word—THINK.

"Why not just say it plainly?" he rebutted.

"You mean take out the word think? But what if I never actually do it?" I almost yelled as my palms started to sweat.

I explained that it felt safe to dream as long as I kept inserting the word think before my goals and wishes. As soon as I took it out, the situation felt more serious. What if I never got the opportunity to write a book? What a failure I would be to say I wanted to write one but never did. I'd be a huge disappointment to myself. But by inserting the word think, no one could ever point to my life and ask me why I never wrote a book. I never said I would, after all—just that I thought I would like to.

"Just say it out loud," he urged.

"Fine. I'd like to write a book someday," I said as I rolled my eyes. I didn't expect anything to happen, but after I said those words to appease Neil, everything felt different. Suddenly writing a book wasn't this wishy-washy idea. It wasn't a hidden idea anymore. It grew legs and came alive! I wanted to write a book! And my heart suddenly wanted to see whether it was possible to string a bunch of coherent words together to create one. I didn't know yet what it would be about, but I enjoyed writing my Better Life Bags blog posts, and I knew that the words I wrote connected with my readers. Maybe I could write a book.

"Well, what will you write about?" Neil asked, taking another bite of his steak.

I thought for a minute about what story I would tell the world if ever given the chance.

"I want to write a book for those women who email and call and visit me with a dream dripping in their hands. I want to write a book and tell them their dream is good and attainable and worth pursuing. But I want them to know they don't have to sacrifice their families or their sleep or their bank accounts to make those dreams come true. I want to show them the highs and lows of running Better Life Bags as an inspiring message of being the turtle—balancing the hustle—and trusting God for the growth."

Neil listened to all this with the most attentive posture and then leaned in close to my ear to whisper, "I can't wait to read the book you write in ten years."

Had he said ten years? Neil had asked me to boldly state something I wanted to do—dared me to dream out loud—and then insinuated I would need to wait ten years before seeing my dream come to life. I wanted to get home and start writing the book now! Ten years seemed like an incredibly long time to wait. Surely I could write a book and see it published within a year if I worked hard enough. I could get up early before the sun and stay up late after the kids went to bed, burning the candle at both ends for the sake of realizing my deepest dreams. But I knew Neil was right. This dream might take ten years or longer to realize and that would be just fine—good even! I didn't need to fall into society's expectations that after I set a goal, I need to start running after it as fast as I can.

I mean, just think about January 1. Pretty much everyone in America sets New Year's resolutions. And almost all of them come with an expiration date—December 31. We sit down and name some goals we would like to accomplish during the upcoming year. Climb Mount Everest. Lose twenty pounds. Write a trilogy. Take a photography class. We list a lot of things. And the stopwatch starts ticking as soon as that ball drops in Times Square. Everyone goes racing off after their midnight kiss to get after their goals.

A quick Google search told me that if you're like 92 percent of those people who set resolutions, you quit working toward them by January 12. Sources showed various percentages and dates of falling off the bandwagon, so we can't be sure of the exact number, but it's obvious that most of the dreams we set for ourselves often fall by the wayside and die a quick death.

What I couldn't find with a Google search was whether any of those resolutions and goals were ever accomplished—even years later. Had anyone fallen off the resolution bandwagon on January 12 but hopped back on in August? How many years did "lose twenty pounds" end up on the top of someone's resolution list before the weight finally came off?

That's what I'd be interested in knowing. I think we would be surprised to see that sometimes many years lie between the birth of a goal and the finish line. Maybe dreams don't die after all—no need to flush them down the toilet—they are just simmering.

Now, I'm definitely not known for my cooking abilities, but I do know a thing or two about simmering. It's a term that means cooking something at just below the boiling point. There's an easy meal my mom made while I was growing up that used a chicken breast, a can of Diet Coke, and a cup of ketchup. That's it. You put the chicken in a frying pan, dump the ketchup and Diet Coke on top, and bring the mixture to a boil before turning down the heat to let it simmer. The sauce looks thin and watery at this point, and you wonder who ever decided to mix ketchup and Diet Coke together. It doesn't look appetizing until thirty minutes—or more—of simmering. The sauce thickens into a nice tasty topping for the rice and chicken. The first time I made this meal on my own, I thought the sauce would never thicken. But after some patience and constant stirring, I ended up with a yummy meal.

A lot of dreams are like this. They need time to simmer. Sometimes a long time.

The other day, while driving my kids around to day camps, guitar practice, and baseball games, I listened to a podcast with Megan Tamte, a co-CEO of the contemporary fashion and styling company EVEREVE. When you glance at the "Our Story" page on their website, it appears that Megan, unhappy with a dressing room experience, had a dream for a new retail experience for women, and then it happened! But when you listen to her interview, you find out that there were five years of doing nothing except dreaming and talking between that dressing room experience and 2004, when they first opened. Five years! Megan mentioned that a few times during those five years, the dream would die a bit. It wouldn't sound as exciting, and she would stop talking about it for a while. But a few months later, something would spark the dream alive again. The dream to create a fashion and retail experience that catered to women in a fresh way wouldn't go away. And eventually, it came to be—after a good simmer.

What do you do if this is your dream—the one that originates in your heart and is begging to get out? How do you let a dream simmer if it's not time to go after it?

While you've got that dream just below the boiling point, keep your ears tuned in to anything that relates to your dream. Let's say you want to lose some weight. Start following Instagram accounts that share healthy recipes and fitness ideas. Maybe you would like to have a hobby farm someday, and as you're driving your kids to school, an interview comes on the radio about someone who raises and breeds chickens for a living. Tune in to that. Dial in to anything that you can find or stumble upon that relates to your dream. Read it. Listen to it. Bookmark it. Take the webinar class. Listen to the podcast.

As long as you think about the dream and still get excited about it, let it keep simmering. Don't turn off the heat, killing your dream, but don't turn the heat up so high that it boils out of control before it's ready. Keep a controlled simmer going for a while, and look for the clues and breadcrumbs—those special stickers stuck to the cement—that will direct you to your next step.

God has had every day of your life planned before you ever took your first breath. It's full of adventure and passion and pain and heartbreak. You can't avoid any of it. It's a journey you don't want to miss and one you can't run from. It's a path you get to uncover as you go, not pave for yourself. Those dreams that won't go away are part of the plan, but it's not up to us to make them come true. They are already true. They are already waiting for you at the finish line. You can't work hard enough or fast enough to reach them. Well, you can, but they won't come any quicker—they come when the time is right—and you'll just be tired. Instead, trust the creator of the universe and the maker of your heart with your dreams. Allow him to show you when to turn the heat up to a boil.

I want to write a book someday. I sat with those words hanging in the air—waiting for something to happen—long after our anniversary date was over.

Then, one summer morning, I woke up to the sun shining in through the cracks in the blinds. My kids had slept in. Thank you, Jesus. I reached for my phone to check my email—the first thing I tend to do every morning.

The subject line "Reaching Out" caught my eye. I opened the email and read:

"Hi Rebecca . . ."

"A friend told me about your business . . ."

"I'm one of the senior marketing directors . . ."

"Have you ever considered writing a book . . ."

"If you're interested . . ."

Someone from a big-name publishing company had emailed me. They wanted to sit down over coffee and talk to me about me writing a book.

I read the email three times before I set down my phone, rested my forehead on top of the smooth screen, and laughed out loud.

"Right now, God? You want me to write it now?" I asked as I thought about how I would fit writing a book into my already full life. That dream was simmering. It wasn't time to write a book—or at least I didn't think it was. I was pregnant with our fourth child and gearing up for my second year of homeschooling Jonah and Clara while Corbin attended the public preschool. Plus, I was running Better Life Bags! Life was full.

"I'm supposed to write this book in ten years, God." I tried to convince him that this was absurd timing. "You know, when I'm almost an empty nester and I've figured out all the world's wisdom. By then Better Life Bags will be a smooth-operating machine, and I'll know all the lessons to pass on. Do you really want me to write this book right now?"

I already knew the answer. This email was another special sticker from God. And so I responded within a few hours. I told the senior marketing director that I would love to sit down over coffee and talk about this possibility. I told her that I'd wanted to write a book for a long time but had been letting that dream simmer and cook a little longer before actively pursuing it. I had been sitting back, writing for fun until the timing was right.

This seemed to be pretty obvious timing. It was time to write a book.

CHAPTER 7

Manage the Hustle

Time to Turn It Up to a Boil

||||||||||||||||||||||||||||||||||||||||||||||||||||||||||||||||||||||||||||||

Once a dream that has been simmering starts to show signs of life, we need to give it a chunk of our time and a little more attention. We need to take intentional steps to walk after and into the plans God has prepared for us. We need to work a little harder and longer, focusing in on the work needed to grow the dream. We need to take our dreams from a simmer to an intentional boil.

This is when many people start to hustle.

Maybe you love to hustle. You love feeling busy and getting after the day, and you feel important when anyone notices how much you accomplish or wonders how you do it all. You wear T-shirts and drink out of coffee mugs that say: "Good things happen to those who hustle." Hustle is not a bad word to you, and you get defensive when anyone suggests that maybe you need to slow down.

Or maybe you hate the word hustle. When you hustle, you feel overly tired, too busy, and as if any success to be had in life is up to you to accomplish—alone. You feel as though hustling means there is no time for rest or play or connecting with those you love. You turn down opportunities meant for you because you feel as though you don't have the time or the margin to do one more thing. You hate feeling rushed. You don't want to hustle.

I have been on both sides of that fence. I don't like to sweat. And I don't like to feel rushed or hurried. If I have the choice to work more or rest more, I'm probably going to choose rest. But I also like to see projects accomplished. It feels good to work hard and meet a goal. I love a good to-do list and checking off the tasks as I go.

Whichever way you lean, take a deep breath. This is for you. I want to show you a third way. A way where you can run a business, write a book, homeschool your kids, keep a tidy house, and still have time to read a book and paint your nails. A way where you can lie in a hammock while you watch your kids play in the backyard and not feel anxious about all those emails waiting to be answered or the to-do list hanging on the fridge. A way where the hustle doesn't control you, but you manage the hustle.

One way to manage the hustle is to set a limit for yourself—a time limit, a word count limit, or a daily limit for the hustle. How long will you hustle after your dream in a given day or week? How much time and energy do you have available to dedicate to it? During the early years of Better Life Bags, I answered emails only on Tuesdays and Thursdays. If it was Monday, I didn't even think about how many emails might be waiting. Monday wasn't an email day, so I focused on other things. Maybe Saturday is laundry day at your house. If so, resist the urge to do laundry on Thursday when the baskets are overflowing. Laundry day is Saturday, and it will all get done then. Another limit that works well for me is to set five-minute timers. If a room is a disaster and I can't focus on anything else, I set a five-minute timer and go to town on that room. I'm moving quick, bending over and scooping up toys, books, lost socks, and dirty underwear and scurrying around to deposit them in their proper locations. When that five-minute timer goes off, I have to stop. I hustled for five minutes—hard—and now I need to move on with the rest of my day.

Now that I had signed a contract with a publisher, I needed to buckle down and do the work. Sixty thousand words were due in eight months. At some point during those eight months, our fourth baby was due to join our family. And I needed to write an entire book.

I needed a limit for myself, or I would constantly be worried about finishing the book on time. I decided I would write one thousand words a day—without fail—until Gavin was born in October. So I did. Some days one thousand words came easy, and other days it was a struggle. But once they were written, I stopped and didn't worry about writing again until the next day.

When Gavin arrived, I strapped his tiny body to my chest and let him sleep to the sound of my fingers typing on the keyboard. Sixty days at one thousand words a day would bring me to sixty thousand words—my first draft. Sometimes those words would be written in chunks while working at home. Other times my husband would send me off to Starbucks to write for an uninterrupted period of time.

On one of these trips, I finished my one thousand words with an hour to spare before I needed to be home to nurse Gavin.

I told myself to keep going. Get ahead! Go further! Hustle! Keep chugging along! I tried, but the words weren't coming as easily as they had been, so I stopped. I saved my document, turned off my headphones, and shut down my computer.

One thousand words had been the goal, and I had reached it. There was no need to keep pushing for more. I walked out of the frigid coffee shop and into the Michigan summer sun, heading straight for my car. I could be home early!

But the sun's rays pulled me to a halt. I looked up at the blue sky and over at the outdoor tables with their large umbrellas that offered inviting shade, and I decided to change course. The cool summer breeze pushed me in the direction of that outdoor retreat. The kids were in capable hands. I still had forty-five minutes before I needed to be home. I could sit here and just rest for at least thirty minutes—maybe even read a chapter of the book I always carry with me in case I ever get time to read.

And so I did. I sat. I read. I closed my eyes and laid my head back on the chair for a few minutes. I almost fell asleep. I could have struggled and pushed through another thousand words, but I knew that if I took this moment to soak in some vitamin D and read a book just for fun, I would come back tomorrow refreshed and ready to pound out another thousand words.

You see, hustle is an overactive ultramarathoner who never runs out of races to run or energy to burn. And unless I sit down and tell the hustle exactly how far he can take me, he will have me signed up for every race this side of the equator. I have to lay down the law with hustle. I have to tell him, "This far and no farther." When hustle comes knocking on my door asking me to go for a run, I don't throw on my running shoes and head out the door right away. But I also don't tell him to leave me alone. When hustle rings my doorbell and tells me it's time to run, I check my calendar and priorities to see whether today is a good day for a jog.

I manage the hustle.

Another way to manage the hustle is to create a series of questions—or boundaries—that help you decide whether to accept hustle's call.

For example, I get a lot of requests for speaking at women's events. Speaking engagements are an amazing way to share the story of Better Life Bags and to connect with customers in a personal and intimate way. But speaking engagements also take me away from my family and from the daily operations of the business. I've decided that while my children are young, I want to be home as much as I can. I don't want to miss the tee-ball games and guitar lessons or the movie nights and birthday parties. When they are home, I want to be home—as much as possible.

So when a speaking engagement opportunity comes across my inbox, I run it through a few filters before jumping on the treadmill to keep up with the hustle:

1. Is the speaking engagement on a weekday at a time when my kids would be occupied with school anyway?
   Yes? Continue on . . .
2. Does it require me to spend the night?
   Yes? Foot off the gas to reevaluate.
   No? Things are looking good. Keep moving forward.
3. Can my family come?
   Yes? Well, this is a no-brainer. A night at a hotel with a swimming pool while I get to explore a new city with my family? Yes, please.
   No? I will probably decline the opportunity.

This hustle filter helps me objectively decide what I should say yes to and what I need to pursue. It's especially helpful if you're introverted and love to stay at home like I do. I hate public speaking. So whenever I'm presented with an opportunity to travel and speak somewhere, I immediately want to say no. It's not that I'm terrible at public speaking. I simply hate doing it. Generally, it feels like a death sentence to me. I kiss my husband goodbye for the last time. I eat my favorite last meal and cry as I think about not seeing my children grow up and graduate or get married. I imagine myself never getting to hold my newborn grandbaby. I leave some final instructions for my family and write "I love you" on the chalkboard in our living room to immortalize my handwriting in case I don't make it out alive. Obviously, the more speaking engagements I accept and come back alive from, the more I realize that this is an irrational fear, but those gut-wrenching nervous feelings about speaking to a group of strangers never leave.

One day a church two hours from me emailed to see whether I would be free to come speak at their women's group on a Tuesday morning. I wanted to say no. No, I didn't want to prepare a message and practice it at home. No, I didn't want to worry about what I would wear or whether my hair would cooperate that day. No, I didn't want to be on stage with a room full of strangers staring at me. No, I didn't want to risk the chance that I would freeze and forget everything I wanted to say. None of that sounded fun.

But after running this speaking opportunity through my decision-making questions, I knew my answer had to be yes. It was during the week, which meant I wouldn't miss out on a weekend with my family. And it was within a two-hour drive, so I could be home by dinnertime. It met my requirements for saying yes to a public speaking engagement.

Interestingly, it was at this event in West Michigan that I met a woman named Barb, a longtime Better Life Bags customer and fan. I didn't know it at the time, but Barb's sister-in-law is the senior marketing director who would eventually contact me about writing a book. Barb was the initial one to bring up my name as a potential author. The inquiry email was sent to my inbox a few months later, and now I sit here writing the book that I always wanted to write. Had I said no to the speaking engagement like I wanted to, this unique opportunity may never have come along.

My self-created parameters help me know when to say yes and when to say no to the hustle. I've never said yes to something after running it through my filter and regretted it. And I've never wondered what I might be missing out on when I said no to something that would have conflicted with my boundaries. I trust that those boundaries and parameters are good and that God is faithful to bring the personal and business growth within them.

The question begs to be answered: When we hustle, whom are we trusting? Are you hustling because you think you can get your sales quota up higher with just a few more hours on the clock? Or are you trusting that even if you don't meet your monthly sales goal, God will still provide? Are you resting because you're being lazy and ignoring the instructions from God to work hard and diligently at your after-school volunteer position? Are you listening to your coach—to God—and running as hard as you can when he's yelling from the sidelines, "Go! Hustle! Run!" And are you listening to him when he tells you to slow down, don't run, and catch your breath?

What if we truly believed God when he told us he has good plans for us? And what if our job is simply to walk faithfully into each step as it's revealed to us—to look for the special stickers and pick them up as we see them? What if we were faithful to work hard when we needed to but also equally valued rest and play? What if we waited more and hustled less? What if we prayed more about our dreams and Instagrammed them less?

I realize this is not popular advice for entrepreneurs. The business coaches and leaders are telling us to work harder and longer—keep grinding and hustling. Work for it more than you hope for it. Hustle until your haters ask whether you're hiring. Beat everyone to the top. And don't quit until you've arrived.

I don't buy into that. I don't think heavy hustling is the only way to success. Perhaps it has meant that Better Life Bags has grown slower than it could have if I'd sacrificed more of my priorities to hustle harder. Maybe we could be a multimillion-dollar company by now. Maybe we could have hundreds of employees with multiple brick-and-mortar locations in lots of cities. Maybe I would have made it onto a Forbes or Inc. business list. But would I have seen my daughter run around the bases at every baseball game? Or lain on the floor with my five-year-old to read his favorite book over and over? Would I have missed the first words of my toddler or the last days of first grade? Maybe. And I couldn't sacrifice that.

We can have both. We can have both the rest and the rewards when we manage the hustle correctly.

Maybe you have a dream of what you want your house to look like—white walls and white trim and hardwood floors and shiplap on accent walls. You scroll Instagram and feel as though everyone else has the house you want. And depending on your personality, you most likely go one of two ways. One way is to ignore everything else in life and get elbow-deep in white paint. You surrender to the hustle and let it take over. Or all the work it will take overwhelms you, and you decide that your house will never look like you want it to, so you don't do anything. You let the hustle take you down.

What if you told the hustle how far it could boss you around? What if you decided to paint just one wall every Saturday? You buy the paint and the brushes and the drop cloth on the first Saturday. On the second Saturday, you whip out the paintbrush and paint and attack just one wall during the baby's naptime and a thirty-minute television show for the other kids.

When that wall is painted, you might look at a second wall and feel as though you have the time to keep going. But don't let the hustle take over. Tell it how far it can go. But no further. Put the paintbrush in a ziplock bag (you don't even need to rinse out the paint), stick it in the fridge, close the paint can, and wait for next Saturday, when you'll have time to make over wall number two. Read a book or magazine if you still have extra time. Before you know it, your whole house will be the perfect shade of white, and it will have gotten done without worry, sweat, or sacrifice of the things that matter most.

We've set up the boundary—this far and no more—and then we trust God for the more.

You are reading this book because I was faithful to sit and do the small work that added up to something big. I hustled for one thousand words a day and then rested. In the middle of writing the first draft, our marketing director at Better Life Bags let me know she had decided to take a job as a nanny and wouldn't be returning. In addition to writing the book and homeschooling my kids, I would now have to resume all marketing efforts at work. It seemed like too much, and I felt defeated—until I set my boundaries for the hustle. I would focus on the VIP Facebook group, Instagram stories, and email marketing. Everything else—monthly lookbooks, photoshoots, and creative Instagram GIFs—would have to stop. That was my limit. And then I trusted God to fill in the gaps.

And he will. He is the ultimate marketer and will bring along the right opportunities for growth, just as he has all along. I don't have to seek them out and exhaust myself in the process. Well, I guess I can. But I don't have to. And I choose more rest over more hustle. More board games. More reading chapter books aloud to my kids. More weekends home on the couch instead of standing behind a table of bags for sale.

I hustle when it's time to hustle, and I rest when it's time to rest.

We don't always need to hustle. We don't need to hurry. Your dreams that just won't die or go away—dreams of writing a book or painting your walls or starting a business—are put there by God, and he has a plan. You don't need to run one hundred miles per hour after the dream, elbowing everyone in your way. But you also don't need to sit on the sidelines and watch everyone else seemingly enjoy their best life without you. You can pursue your dreams under the umbrella of God's guidance and approval. Take small steps one at a time, and you'll get there surprisingly faster and more rested than you ever imagined.

He is good, friends. His path for us is good. It's okay to just walk on it. You don't have to run.

CHAPTER 8

Don't Do It Alone

Because It's More Fun Than Being by Yourself—and Face It . . . You Need Help

||||||||||||||||||||||||||||||||||||||||||||||||||||||||||||||||||||||

As Better Life Bags grew bigger and we hired more people to help make the operation run smoothly, I found myself in the role of CEO. I was not trained for this. Yet I felt the quiet nudge to learn all I could about how to run a business and be a boss.

One of the first—and best—books I read on growing your company was The E Myth. My biggest takeaway from the book was to work on your business instead of in it. The concept made so much sense to me. If Better Life Bags was going to grow and dig its roots down deep for stability, I needed to stop sewing. I needed to focus on new designs, new customers, and new markets and let others do the sewing.

Nadia was hired first—her story becoming the backbone of the company and solidified our mission to hire women who had barriers to traditional employment. Orders kept coming in, so I hired five more seamstresses over the next year—Umme, Roushanara, Shaheda, Ruma, and Parul. If you've ever ordered a bag, you likely recognize one of those names from the "made by" card that comes with every bag. This card tells you who made your bag and why your purchase was important. Customers tell us that they keep that card—hang it on their fridge—and think about the maker of their bag every time they look at it. The cards have been such a fun way to connect the customer to the woman who made her bag, and a few customers have even written personal thank-you cards back to their seamstresses.

Karima, the seventh seamstress we hired, has multiple thank-you notes hanging from her bulletin board next to her sewing machine in the workshop. Handing a piece of mail to a seamstress or reading her a positive review from the website about a bag she made has become one of my favorite parts of working at Better Life Bags. Our seamstresses are loved so well by our customers, and it thrills me that a customer knows the name of the woman who made their bag and can personally thank her for her work.

Karima joined our team in late 2015. Sometime in the fall of that year, Neil had been driving home from a leather pickup at Tandy Leather. We were buying forty hides of leather a month at this point—sometimes even more around the holidays—and I needed to think about whom our next hire would be. Neil would often make our leather runs for us, lifting heavy hides into our car and delivering them to our workshop. While he was driving, his radio was always turned to NPR.

"From WBEZ Chicago, it's This American Life. I'm Ira Glass."

The episode was highlighting people who have made big transformations, and Neil's ears perked up when he heard "Detroit." Ira Glass was following a woman who was about to use Detroit's public transportation for the first time. She was new to America, having arrived from Afghanistan a few months before. Returning to her country would put her life in danger, and America was the safe refuge she needed.

She was staying in Detroit at a temporary home for asylum seekers called Freedom House. They taught her how to put together a resume, shop at grocery stores, find a doctor, and today, she would learn how to take the bus.

As they journeyed together through Detroit, Ira Glass asked her what she hoped to do in America. She had recently received her legal paperwork to get a job, but looking for work had landed nothing.

"She's a college grad with a bachelor's in business administration," his voice boomed over the radio speakers. "Back home in Kabul, she did project management for an international organization—humanitarian projects. It's not unusual, of course, but this immigrant who's used to a job in her own country managing things and doing PowerPoint presentations and looking at Excel spreadsheets is hoping that here in America she'll get work as a seamstress if she's lucky."

Neil shut off the radio and called me. "There's a woman in Detroit. They didn't say her name. But she needs a job. She's looking for a sewing position. You should hire her!"

I had no idea how to contact her. To protect her privacy, they didn't even say her name on the radio. They just called her "M." A few weeks later, an email popped into my inbox. "My name is Karima, and I'm forty-two. I am an asylum seeker, living in a shelter called Freedom House in Detroit. . . . I have experience of sewing for over twenty years. I am seeking for a job. . . . Please help me if you have job available by replying to this email."

I wondered whether it could be the same asylum seeker

that Neil heard on NPR. I invited her in for an interview and asked whether she had been on This American Life. She had. This was the same woman!

The way God was adding people to Better Life Bags was amazing. He was bringing the people he wanted to work there to our door.

While I had passed a lot of the actual work of sewing off to our amazing seamstresses, I was still answering customer emails, printing off orders, cutting fabric and leather, shipping the bags, designing new bag styles, training seamstresses, and doing the social media, which at the time was our only source of marketing.

And at this point in the company's timeline, I was expecting baby number three, and we had recently bought our house and were frantically fixing it up before the baby came. My days of working forty to fifty hours a week were coming to an end, and I was forced to think about replacing myself and finding someone to run the day-to-day operations of the business—at least until I settled into the role of being a mom of three.

I not only wanted to be able to take a maternity leave for at least three weeks without shutting down the business, but I also missed spending more time with my other two kids who were three and four years old already. They were growing faster than the weeds in our office parking lot, and I realized how much I had missed of their little lives while I had been focusing on growing the business to a place where it would support our family financially. I didn't want to miss any more moments. I wanted to stay home more and invest in their little hearts as I'd always dreamed of doing.

When I quit my teaching job after finding out I was pregnant with our first child, I was so excited to fulfill my lifelong dream of being a stay-at-home mom. And then I made a diaper bag—accidentally starting a business—and my stay-at-home mom status was never fully realized.

I wasn't upset about any of this. I was grateful for the creative outlet the business provided. But I wanted to explore the option of putting someone in place to run the day-to-day operations of Better Life Bags so I could be home more. I wanted to cook macaroni and cheese while designing a new bag in my head and to snuggle on the couch and watch a movie while creating a social media marketing campaign. So much of my job could also easily be done from home when I wasn't preoccupied and worried about the actual products being made. I hoped hiring someone to take point on the daily operations would also free me up to be a more present mom.

For this to happen, I would need to hire a full-time operations manager to keep the day-to-day activities going within the business. And it needed to be someone who was willing to take a meager starting salary since I would be sharing a portion of my own tiny salary with her.

I wasn't sure I could find someone willing to do a lot of work for very little pay and love the company as much as I did. But if anyone could, I knew it would be Elise. She had been volunteering her time for over a year, sewing straps for each bag, and had an up-front view of everything that happened in the business. She knew the bags and she knew our seamstresses. She had moved to Hamtramck for reasons similar to ours. Her daughter lived here and started an English as a second language program and a women's fitness center that Elise wanted to help with. She was perfect for the operations manager job—very detail oriented and fiercely loyal.

Except she already had a job. When she wasn't sewing straps for our bags, she worked as a math tutor a few cities away from Hamtramck. I knew taking this position would be a huge pay cut for her, but I also knew we could offer "benefits" such as a job with flexible hours down the street from her house so she could help her daughter launch her nonprofit. I had my fingers crossed. Tight.

After two long weeks of considering the job, she accepted the position.

With Elise in place as operations manager, I had successfully taken myself out of the daily tasks of the company. Now I could focus on the future and growth and long-term business plans—which is a bit like playing Monopoly with your eyes closed and gloves on. I had no idea what I was doing or how to steer this ever-growing ship toward success. But at least now I had a little more margin to focus on the future.

I gave birth to a business that needed full-time attention to keep growing. But I was also having physical babies of my own whom I wanted to raise, and inviting Elise to run the operations side of the business allowed me to do both. I'm forever indebted to her and grateful for her brave yes—for taking a risk, listening to God's direction, and jumping in as the most loving and protective business nanny I ever could have found. I now felt the freedom to enjoy my maternity leave and stay home most days to be with my kids.

A few years after relinquishing control over Better Life Bags's day-to-day operations and focusing instead on bag designs and product marketing, I felt the nudge to hire again. I wanted to find someone to train our seamstresses and coach them on quality standards. It was the next area of business that needed to be taken off Elise's and my plates.

This new hire I was imagining also needed to be an expert

seamstress, ideally having worked in the sewing business before. I needed someone who could take new bag designs from my head and create prototypes for me to look at. I had so many ideas and not enough time to flesh them out.

The biggest stumbling block was that this person needed to live in Hamtramck or Detroit and have a heart for ministry to different cultures. I sat down with Elise one morning and spelled everything out to her. With a big sigh, I leaned back in my chair and ended with, "Unfortunately, that person doesn't exist here in Hamtramck."

A few weeks later, I got a text from a friend from the neighborhood: "I have someone you need to meet. She needs to work for you."

And a few weeks after that, Jennifer walked through our doors and into the family of Better Life Bags. Not only had she owned her own sewing business in the past, but she was also highly skilled in clothing alterations—specifically with leather. After her business closed its doors, she was a server for the next decade or two. She was ready to quit the restaurant world but had no idea what was next. And guess what? She lived only a few blocks from my house in Hamtramck. She'd been here all along!

Jennifer started working at Better Life Bags one Friday morning a week—before her restaurant shift—until I presented her with a full-time job offer. I couldn't believe how gracious God was to bring her to us, especially after I was so sure such an individual didn't exist in our city. I imagined God looking down, hearing me saying that and smiling, knowing whom he was about to bring into our lives.

Everything had grown so quickly that being forced to hire more and more people to help me do the jobs I no longer could keep up with was such a blessing. And you know what? They were better at those jobs than I ever was! I found this out one year when Nadia was having baby number five.

We wanted her to be able to spend her first few weeks postpartum bonding with her new little baby instead of worrying about her workload. So I offered to fill in and make all of Nadia's bags for her while she was on maternity leave.

It was strange to sit down at the sewing machine again and try to remember how to make the bags I had designed. Since I had stopped sewing bags, Jennifer had come in with her expertise and shown everyone how to do a lot of operations more efficiently, so a lot about how we made our bags had changed from back when it was only me, a sewing machine, a sleeping baby, and a quiet apartment.

I found out years later that Jennifer remade every bag I made when Nadia was on maternity leave. My sewing wasn't good enough anymore! I really had worked myself out of a job. I was so glad at that moment that I had hired Jennifer.

Finding help didn't mean I had failed. If you need help cleaning your house, for goodness sake, hire a cleaning service. That will free you up to do things in your life that only you can do—without sacrificing the cleanliness of your home. If you are building a business or writing a blog and need uninterrupted hours of the day, please hire a babysitter—or trade babysitting duties with a friend. You are not a terrible mom for doing so. You will be a more present mom when you're with your kids because you will not be trying to work on your dream while chasing babies at the same time.

This team coming together around Better Life Bags was so crucial to its success. Each woman worked alongside me day after day to create the bags our customers ordered, and we were building a better life together.

On any given weekday, you could walk in the front doors

of 9411 Joseph Campau Street in Hamtramck and be met with the distinct smell of leather. You would hear the sewing machines humming as you stepped into the retail section of our workshop. Sample bags hang on the wall so you could touch and smell and try on each style, and embroidery hoops filled with our fabric selections for you to choose from hang next to them. If you walked around the wall jutting out halfway to separate the retail space from the workshop, you'd see Jubilee. She cuts every piece of fabric needed for that week's orders of bags—opening and closing deep wooden drawers that hold our fabric bolts as she goes. Sabah, our leather cutter who walked into our workshop one day to ask for change for the parking meter outside, is next to her. She was headed to apply for a seamstress job at the alterations spot on the corner. We took her number down just in case that job didn't pan out and called her a few weeks later for an interview!

A table is set up with two sewing machines on it—waiting for Roushanara and Shaheda to come sit twice a week and chat while they sew the cotton dust bags that orders are shipped in. Jennifer and Karima sit across from each other at our industrial sewing machines—the ones that make that soothing hum you hear. They both work full-time—guaranteed to be here no matter what day or time you walk in. Elise has her computer set up off to their right, but she's rarely just sitting. She's a busy bee, rushing all around the workshop as she double-checks Jubliee's and Sabah's fabric and leather pieces before they are sent home to the seamstresses. She still sews quite a bit to finish out the bags when they come back. And she prints off orders as they come in and divvies them out to the appropriate seamstress, makes sure they get sewn together the way the customer designed them, and ensures that they're finished on time. If your order is going to be late or we have a question about a design aspect that you chose, Elise would likely be the one to email you. She runs the entire shop.

Our shipping department is in the back of our workshop. Right now Elizabeth commands this space. In addition to quality-checking every single bag before it's shipped, she uses a soldering iron to melt down any loose threads around the bag. Before the leather pieces are sent out to our seamstresses, Elizabeth uses a four-hundred-degree arbor press to brand our logo into the side.

I've loved watching God bring all the right people at the right time. We all need each other to do our jobs and keep the company running. I came to realize that, as it is with most tasks that become too large for one person, it takes a team. Each team member has a distinct and important role that makes the whole operation run. When one person is missing or sick or on vacation, we all feel the void.

This idea of replacing ourselves and not going about it alone is not only a concept for business. It applies to everyday life too. It even applies to being a mom. While you will always be a mom to those sweet children of yours, someday they aren't going to need you anymore. And they won't need you because you trained them to do everything you used to do for them—wipe their bottoms, make a healthy dinner, save money, do laundry, drive a car, get a job. You've modeled how to raise a family, and someday your kids may imitate you and do the same.

This is success. Our kids growing up and leaving our nests as competent adults is a high-five. A job well done, Mama.

When I was in college learning how to be an effective teacher, my biggest takeaway was discovering how to create a classroom with rules and procedures that essentially ran without me. If I was late to school one day, no one should even realize it (much!) because the kids in my classroom would know exactly how to start their day. I've carried this lesson into my family and my work. A better life is one that can run without my orchestrating every task or decision and bossing everyone around. The people in my life—my children included—know their roles and their jobs, and they wake up and do them. My eight-year-old daughter does one load of laundry a day. My nine-year-old son empties the dishwasher. I'm in the process of replacing myself at home. Because life works better when we all pitch in. And because Mama needs a break!

The most humbling part about replacing ourselves is that it reminds us that we are not the center of the universe. We are not the sun. Life does not revolve around us. And we cannot do it all. We need other people. We need a team. We weren't meant to do everything on our own. Often other people can do something better than we can, and we need to let them. We can delegate and hire and collaborate and work together to accomplish more than if we were alone.

Being surrounded by people—that is a better life. And a better life is when people are invited in—to the mess, to the dream, and to the celebrations. It's when we decide to step aside from trying to do it all ourselves and let others join. It's a life in which we share in the successes and lift each other up during the failures. A better life is one in which we realize what we are doing is significantly less important than whom we are doing it with and what we are doing it for.

CHAPTER 9

Practice Your U-Turns

What to Do When You Realize You're Going the Wrong Way

|||||||||||||||||||||||||||||||||||||||||||||||||||||||||||||||||||||||||||||||||

I was shopping for embroidery thread at JOANN one afternoon in 2015. I was trying my hand at a new hobby since my old hobby had been hijacked into a business. I figured embroidery might be fun to try. This landed me in the thread aisle, completely overwhelmed by all the choices and techniques and options.

"Rebecca Smith?" I heard as I was bent over trying to read the tiny numbers that coincided with each color of floss. Who could that be? I'm way outside Hamtramck city limits. Who else could know my name?

Quite flustered, with my hands full of embroidery floss, I looked up and stared at the face in front of me. I had absolutely no idea who she was. Clueless.

"Ummm, hi?" I said, flabbergasted at how this stranger could know my name.

"This is probably strange, but I follow you and Better Life Bags on Instagram and just love your company!"

Sure enough, I looked down at her hip and she had a navy herringbone print on a Cyndi bag. A Better Life Bag! In the wild! Being carried by someone who wasn't related to me! This was insane!

We chatted calmly for a bit while my insides were going off like fireworks. People were choosing to spend their money on a bag that we made in Hamtramck. And the business was getting big enough that people I didn't even know were ordering. Names that I didn't recognize were coming in attached to orders. Then names came through that friends of friends didn't recognize. We started shipping bags to cities I had never been to and countries I couldn't even pronounce. Word of mouth was spreading news about our company far and wide.

This was definitely more than a hobby. People you don't know don't carry around the by-products of a hobby. This was a business. And I felt out of my league. I had never run a business before—other than lemonade stands when I was ten.

I had been listening to as many books and podcasts about business and marketing as I could. And I loved it all, but the responsibility of this weighed heavily on me. I worried I would mess everything up and become buried alive underneath an enormous pile of fabric and leather scraps. I felt as if I had found myself driving a car one hundred miles per hour on the interstate before I had even gotten my driver's license. Someone else needed to take control of this car before I crashed into the median.

I researched business coaches and how to hire a CEO. I ultimately was connected with a guy in Atlanta who had worked with multimillion-dollar companies and turned massive profits for them. Finally, I had found someone who would hold my hand and walk me through the day-to-day of this avalanche I had started.

We hopped on a phone call, and I explained our massive growth for the past few years—tripling revenue in 2013, doubling in 2014, and on track for doubling again in 2015. I had no idea how we were doing that, but it was starting to feel like a game of hot potato, and I needed to find someone to toss it to before it exploded in my hands.

During our phone call, he flattered me quite a bit. He told me how impressive it was that I had been able to grow a company this quickly.

"Women love their tchotchkes, after all," he said.

The first time he referred to our custom leather and fabric bags as tchotchkes—small knickknacks or trinkets—I let it go. I didn't blame him for not knowing fashion terms and jargon. But it came up multiple times in our conversation.

"I mean, my wife just loves her tchotchkes."

"You can sell all sorts of tchotchkes to women nowadays."

I became offended. These bags weren't knickknacks collecting dust on my grandma's bookshelf. These were high-end handmade items that had an amazing story connected to them.

But this guy knew business. He had credentials up the wazoo. I felt as if I had to trust him because he was the one who could save this venture from being an absolute disaster. He could teach me how to run a business.

When we started talking about how he would be paid for his consulting services, he asked for 10 percent of the sales each month. That was more than I was making! But again, he had the credentials and the degrees and the experience. I didn't even have a business degree. I felt as though all I had done was create a Frankenstein monster that I was afraid was going to turn on me.

I agreed to the terms, and we started our weekly phone calls. Actually, we got through only one phone call before I pulled a fast U-turn and whipped myself right around.

This guy may have gone to school for business, but he didn't know my business. And no number of phone calls would ever convince him that my bags weren't tchotchkes and that we sold so much more than a bag.

I remember pulling up in front of my house after a long day at work and telling myself that I couldn't go inside until I called him. I rolled down my window and turned off the car, feeling the immediate rush of summer heat blowing in my face. I needed to call him right then, before another day went by. This wasn't the right way to spend 10 percent of our sales each month, and my gut knew it. Even if I was desperate to share the weight of responsibility with someone else, it couldn't be Mr. Tchotchke.

"I've made a mistake," I explained after he picked up. "I can't—in good conscience—spend 10 percent of our sales on your salary."

What I didn't tell him that day was that he gave me a boost of confidence in my ability to run my own company. I had been explaining social media marketing to him to get him up to speed on how our customers were finding out about us. I researched a little bit about an influencer he suggested we partner with, only to find out that her blog and Facebook had minimal engagement, and her YouTube videos had less than twenty-five views each. Plus, she ran a "deals site" for women who were into couponing. I knew this wasn't our audience and was surprised he didn't.

His response to my list of reasons why I didn't think this was the person for us to partner with was, "Excellent analysis. That's the last time I throw a referral from someone out there before I check it out."

I *did* know a lot about how to run this business. My gut hadn't let me down before, and this confirmed that it would continue to lead me down the right path. And while the reality that my decisions determined the future of the company was daunting and kept me up at night, it was my company, and only I knew what it needed.

He was gracious in backing off, thankfully. I took a big deep breath, rolled up my window, opened the car door, and walked into my house one hundred pounds lighter. The next day at work, I walked in with a skip in my step and a renewed spirit—the confidence that I really could make decisions in the best interest of this ever-growing giant of a monster I had created. I could make decisions to keep going forward, and I could also decide to swing a U-turn if I ever thought we were going in the wrong direction. The truth is, I'm not a fortune-teller, and I can't see into the future. Often I don't know if a direction or decision was right or wrong until I start walking down the path. Outcomes are impossible to know ahead of time. But with each step after a decision, I decide and discern whether I should keep going or turn around. Hardly anything is permanent and can't be reversed. Almost everything can get back on track with a simple U-turn.

Have you ever committed to a Whole30 program right when Girl Scout Cookie season starts? Before you know it, an entire sleeve of Thin Mints has disappeared—and you don't even know how it happened. This is when you need to U-turn around. Hide the other sleeve, give it away, do something drastic with it, and get back on track. Or maybe you yelled and screamed at your crazy children because they insisted on squawking like ducks starting at 5:30 a.m.—before your first cup of coffee. Your entire day isn't ruined because of one small outburst. You can turn this around. Maybe you went to college for an accounting degree, graduated, landed a great job as a CPA but now want to poke your eyes out from boredom every day. It was a mistake. You realize that you hate numbers. It's not too late to go back to school and get a different degree. It might take another four years, but isn't that better than forty more of doing something you hate?

Wouldn't it be worse to get to the end of your life, look back, and wish that you could do it over again—but better? I don't want that for any of us. Making a mistake with a decision is not the end of the world. Changing your mind does not make you a failure, and it doesn't mean you've wasted time. You don't need to start over. You don't have to return all the way back to "Go." When we're driving and miss our turn on the road, we don't drive all the way home and start the route over. That would be crazy. We make the quickest and soonest turnaround and get right back on the correct course. We can do this with our lives, dreams, and goals too. I personally have stopped viewing my life as one long straight line with a beginning and an end but instead as a journey full of twists and turns, starts and stops, hills and valleys—and yes—U-turns.

| | | | | | | | | | | | | | | | | | | | | | | | | | | | | | | | | | | | | | | | | | | | | | | | | | | | | | | | | | | | | | | | | | | | | | | | | |

Maybe it would be helpful for me to outline a few more of the U-turns I've made at Better Life Bags—just to prove that they are possible and that they don't set us back as much as we think they will.

A few times a year, I'll get an email from an enthusiastic customer or fan of Better Life Bags. They want to know whether they can replicate BLB in their city—specifically with a franchise. It always gets my wheels turning and oils up the big dream section of my brain.

One opportunity in particular seemed very appealing. There was a community similar to Hamtramck in a neighborhood of Atlanta, Georgia—a lot of refugees with similar barriers to employment. A bag company had decided to close its doors, and there was an opportunity to step in and take over its operations.

We held quite a few phone calls with people in Atlanta that had connected us with this bag company. They were mission-minded and were painting this beautiful picture of the community of Clarkston, Georgia, as well as the women who lived there. I wanted to make this happen! We could double the size of Better Life Bags! I couldn't wait to send the email to our customers with the news that Better Life Bags was expanding to its second city.

But I knew we had a lot of details to figure out before that email could be launched out to inboxes everywhere. The biggest detail was who would run the operations in Georgia. My contact there didn't want to, and I wasn't at a point where I could leave Hamtramck just yet. The business needed me here right now. I could leave for a few months to train someone, but that operation needed to run independently of me. And I needed to trust this person. We asked around to anyone we knew who lived near Atlanta or would want to move there and couldn't find anyone.

But it wasn't only the personnel issue that we ran into. The further I walked into this idea of franchising Better Life Bags in a new city, the more I realized it didn't make sense operationally. We didn't want to duplicate operations in two cities and take half the work away from the seamstresses in Hamtramck. It also didn't make sense to have double the machines, supplies, and workforce making the same bags. If we added a new leather color in Hamtramck, we'd need to also order it for Georgia.

I loved and valued how quickly we could make design changes at Better Life Bags. We could add new fabrics, new leathers, or launch a new bag style within weeks—something that would take a normal fashion company months or even years to execute. This was the benefit of sourcing, manufacturing, and selling all under one roof. We could pivot quickly.

Duplicating operations in another city would take this away and make it much harder. The pivots would be much bigger and take a lot longer. Franchising would be a big risk. It could greatly expand our operations and reach. Or it might kill us.

After walking down the road of possibility for a bit—entertaining meeting after meeting to discuss details—I decided to turn around. We weren't ready for this right now.

I refocused back to the women in our city and decided to dig deeper and make sure I was doing the best job with the workshop and the women I had been given. If duplicating Better Life Bags in another city was part of the larger plan, then I knew more pieces of the puzzle would fall into place at the right time. It wasn't something I needed to push for or force into fruition. For now, we would stay as one workshop space in the middle of Detroit, Michigan.

Each U-turn I've made at Better Life Bags has helped to define and nail down the focus of our business—what we make and how we make it. Saying no to franchising in different cities meant we focused our attention on being a local Detroit business. It helped clarify who we hire. But sometimes I find myself resistant to change, doing things the same way just because it's the way we've always done it. Knowing that businesses need to move and change in order to grow, I consider every opportunity or inquiry that comes across my email as a potential new step for us, a sticker showing me the next move. For example, when boutiques that specialized in and focused on ethical and fair-trade fashion started emailing to ask if they could wholesale our products to sell in their stores, I considered it. Maybe this would be the next stream of revenue for us. Most product-based businesses wholesale their products; maybe we should too.

So we started. We created wholesale line sheets and minimum order quantities. And we took on our first five wholesale customers. We figured out how to ship multiple bags at once and how to collect payment. And we doubled our efforts to make twice as many bags for half the price.

Yep. Wholesale means that you offer your products at half the price so the boutique can make a profit as they resell them at full retail price. The idea is that the higher volume ideally makes the discount worth it.

Except that wasn't how our company was set up. We didn't create bags in mass quantities. We specialized in custom products and made them to order. We didn't need to push product or hold on to inventory because we didn't have inventory to push. Everything we were making and working on had already sold, and customers were patiently waiting for them to arrive.

Wholesale meant we were working harder for less money. Sure, there were some marketing opportunities to think about. We were getting our bags in boutiques across the country for customers to go visit and see in person. But I wanted those customers to buy from us and our website. I wanted to invest in them and get to know them as people. I couldn't be sure that the boutiques would tell our story well. And part of the beauty of Better Life Bags has been the direct connection with our customers.

Wholesale didn't make sense.

So we U-turned. We stopped.

I've also walked down the road of turning Better Life Bags into a company that has ambassadors and home parties and the like. Two of the companies Better Life Bags has grown up alongside have structured their businesses this way. And I wondered how many more bags we could sell if we allowed some of our best and most enthusiastic customers to become ambassadors for us and sell on our behalf.

I opened applications for ambassadors, and responses flooded in. I was honored and floored by how many women wanted to sell Better Life Bags in their communities.

This could work!

But the logistics behind it all felt like Mount Everest to climb. It started off easy—find and hire ambassadors. But then it quickly snowballed. How do we pay them? How do we get them product to sell? How do we receive their custom orders from their parties? How do we coach these women and give them the tools they need to be successful and feel supported?

We had to stop. The energy we were exerting meant we would need to hire an additional team member to run this part of the operation. And I had built Better Life Bags up until that point without any debt or loans or an outside investment. I liked the grassroots feel of it and not owing anyone anything. I wasn't ready to expand in this way.

I U-turned again. And we settled back into finding customers, making bags, sending them out, and hiring women from our community.

Wholesaling and home parties could have easily turned out as successful as that small ask to add leather to a bag. So as I did with the leather, I started walking down that road to feel it out a little more. But after testing those ideas, I realized they weren't the right decisions for us.

Probably the most important U-turn I've made in the life of Better Life Bags happened two years into our move to Hamtramck. If you remember, we were only planning to live in Hamtramck for a few years. We would learn a language, get used to being surrounded by various cultures, and then make the leap overseas to fulfill God's call on our lives—or at least what we thought at the time was God's purpose for us—to reach unreached people groups in Asia with the gospel.

Our time in Hamtramck was coming to an end, and we had been accepted to a practicum in Amman, Jordan, that would teach us fluent Arabic in just two years. Normally, they didn't accept families with children, but they made an exception for us, and we prepared to move overseas with two small children, bringing my brother along to help with the kids and to free me up for language learning.

I wasn't sure what this meant for Better Life Bags. I hadn't hired anyone yet, so it was still very much a hobby that could be put on hold at any moment. I knew it would mean a pause on any sewing and shipping of product—my Etsy shop would be put on vacation mode—but I had heard about a missional business in Amman that made products out of olive wood and hired men and women with disabilities to make them. In addition to my language learning, I hoped to learn from and apprentice under the owners to see if Better Life Bags could someday do something similar in another part of Asia.

We had all but bought the tickets. But something was stopping us. Every day, we would wake up and feel unsettled about the idea of moving to Jordan. It didn't make sense because this had been the plan all along. We should feel excited and ready to go! Instead, we felt as though we were leaving a project unfinished. So despite all the planning and preparations, we decided to stay. It was kind of embarrassing, actually. Family and friends all expected us to make the big move—some had even offered to help support us financially—and it looked as if we were backing out. We wondered whether people would assume we were too scared to go, chickening out by staying in Hamtramck instead. But we knew deep down that the right decision was to stay here and see what the unfinished work was.

It didn't take long to find out. The very month we should have been starting our Arabic lessons in Jordan was the very month that Joy Cho pinned that black-and-white laptop bag on her Pinterest board—sending hundreds of orders our way and launching Better Life Bags into its first massive growth spurt. Had we gone to Jordan, we would have missed it. My bag-making hobby would have been "on vacation," and all those potential customers would have walked away empty-handed. Instead, because we U-turned from our original plan when things felt uneasy, we found ourselves off running on the greatest adventure of our lives.

CHAPTER 10

Don't Be Afraid to Fail

It's Really Not as Bad as You Think

||||||||||||||||||||||||||||||||||||||||||||||||||||||||||||||||||||||

One time we had a customer email to ask whether we really hired women from our community or whether everything was fake—just a ploy to get people to feel good about buying bags. They were rightfully questioning us because they never see our seamstresses on Instagram, and their stories are not the public spectacle that one might expect from a company with a mission such as ours. But this is not without reason.

The Bible instructs in Matthew 6:1 not to do our good deeds publicly in order to be admired by others. But the previous chapter in Matthew tells us to let our light shine before others so they will see our good works and glorify God. This has been a tricky balance for Better Life Bages. The foundation of the company is this idea that we invest deeply in the lives of our employees and provide a better life for them. I need to share about the good we are doing because it closely relates to our sales and our marketing. But at the same time, I choose to share only a fraction of what goes on behind the bags. Our mission is to hire women with barriers to employment. Sometimes this barrier can be embarrassing or shameful, and the story isn't ours to share. Sometimes sharing more about the women who work for us would endanger their lives, especially the ones seeking refuge in America. And most of the time, we don't share the struggles and triumphs of the women who work for us because their culture or their family would prefer their names and faces remain private. We get creative when we can by showing pictures of hands or the backs of their heads, but most important to me is that the women who sew for us feel as though Better Life Bags is a safe place to be. Their comfort is more important than a marketing plan.

So most of our mission is conducted in secret, behind closed doors, off social media. But that email really got to me. I couldn't get her words off my mind. I wondered how many other potential customers thought we might be lying about our mission just to pull at emotional heartstrings and make a sale. It became important to me to prove them wrong.

While most of our employees weren't able to have their pictures shown or stories told, there was one who didn't mind sharing her story and life with our customers—Casandra. Remember the day she came into our workshop and our seamstresses told me they were scared? Yet how they overcame stereotypes and false beliefs to embrace someone from a different race as their friend? Well, Casandra was our employee with the most need. She was the one I really wanted to save so I could prove to myself and to our customers that we really do make lives better. She would be the proof.

I met her on the first warm day of 2014. She was out

walking her baby, and I was out doing the same, finally glad for some sunshine in Michigan. I smiled at her as we passed each other on the cracked and broken sidewalks of Hamtramck. She smiled and then stopped me.

"Do you have any extra change? I need to get my baby some diapers," she said.

I had come to the decision that when I come across a person in need—which happens a lot in our city—I would avoid giving money as often as possible. If I can figure out what the actual need is, I try to fill that physical need instead of handing out cash. Casandra needed diapers. I had diapers. This was an easy one. I got her phone number and address and told her I'd drop some off later that evening.

As promised, I pulled up to her house—just a mile from mine—and handed over the box of diapers. When she asked for my phone number so we could take our kids to the park together some time, I happily handed it over. Who knew where this would lead, but connecting with another mother in my city seemed to be the right choice.

That night, as I tucked my three sweet kids into bed, my phone rang. It was Casandra, asking me whether I could give her some money for the bus so she could go donate plasma the next day.

Did you know you can get between fifty and sixty dollars to donate your plasma? I didn't even know what plasma was until Casandra asked me for money that night.

As mentioned before, I don't like to give money if I can meet the actual physical need, so I offered to give her a ride to the plasma center the next day.

I kind of wondered at this point whether Casandra was really a mother in need—or whether she was just trying to get a couple of dollars out of me in any way she could. So I put her to the test. I told her that I could take her to the plasma center the next day, but we would have to leave at 4:30 a.m. so I could be back in time to get my kids to school. Surely if she wasn't truly in need, she would never agree to such an outrageous wake-up time.

But she did. So I figured her need for money outweighed her need for sleep. And we all know how much we mothers need our sleep!

Here entered the biggest problem: I didn't want to wake up at 4:30 a.m. to drive Casandra to the plasma center. I decided to try something different. I called Casandra back and told her I would talk to my boss the next day and see whether she could get her a few hours of work at Better Life Bags cutting leather scraps instead. I'm not sure why I told her I'd consult with my boss when I was the actual boss. I guess it stemmed back to the time when I was tucking Jonah into bed the night before his birthday. He asked whether I had to work the next day, and I told him I didn't because I was the boss and could have his birthday off if I wanted. He promptly reminded me in his sweet little voice, "No, Mama. You're not the boss. God is the boss." And the next day, I changed my business cards from "CEO of Better Life Bags" to "Steward of What God Has Done"—all thanks to that little reminder about who is actually the boss.

Turns out both bosses thought it would be a good idea for Casandra to come cut leather for a few hours instead of donating plasma. And her first day turned into four years.

Better Life Bags was the first job Casandra had ever had. It took some training and some coaching on how to conduct yourself at a job—call when you'll be late, clock out if you have to take a long phone call, and then put the phone away while you work. She started cutting leather scraps down into usable pieces, and then we trained her to cut the fabric for our bags. She had to know every piece for every bag—literally hundreds of measurements—and which way to cut the pattern to utilize the fabric efficiently. She became one of the best and most competent fabric cutters we had ever had. We relied on her heavily to cut the right pieces, and she never let us down. At work she excelled. Outside of work, her life was in constant chaos.

I wanted to change Casandra's life. I wanted to take her situation and turn it into a Cinderella story. I wanted Better Life Bags to have such an impact on her heart and her finances that her life before would be almost unrecognizable. And I wanted to be able to say that Better Life Bags had done this for her.

But it wasn't that easy. She was part of a poverty culture. And expecting her to become a middle-class white woman was frankly racist and ignorant of me. But I tried anyway. I tried setting her up with budgets and payment plans. Yet she was never able to pay her rent on time and was evicted three times in four years. Better Life Bags bailed her out every time, fronting the first and last month's rent over and over in order to keep a roof over her head.

We enrolled her kids in daycare and drove them to and from the daycare center every morning and afternoon. We also covered her late payments and eventually took over the payments altogether so her kids could remain in daycare. If her kids didn't go to daycare, Casandra couldn't go to work. If she couldn't work, she couldn't afford daycare and rent, and the cycle of whatever this was would continue.

One summer, anticipating her older two children being out of school—they were too young to stay home alone and too old for daycare—I put out a cry for babysitting help on our

Better Life Bags Facebook page. Two local families—two of our customers—raised their virtual hands as willing to help. The idea was that they would care for the kids day and night during the week so Casandra could work full days. And then they would bring them back on the weekends so the kids could be with their mama. Everyone was excited about it, including Casandra.

The kids had a blast that summer. And Casandra got to work. Finally, something was working out—until she showed up to work one day in March with another eviction notice. I gave up. I couldn't help her again—or anymore. I didn't have any more leads on places for her to stay, and honestly, I was tired of trying and seeing no change in her life. The local low-income housing complex had a three- to five-year waitlist. So did all of the women's shelters in the area. There was nowhere for her to go, and the countdown clock had started on her thirty-day eviction notice.

At this point, I felt as though we had failed Casandra. It felt time to admit that we really weren't actually making anyone's life better. Especially not Casandra's.

I surrendered. Waved my white flag. Told God I was done helping.

The weight of where those four sweet kids were going to sleep haunted me at night. I pictured them freezing on the side of the road or standing on street corners begging for money. And I felt as though their futures fell on my shoulders. If I didn't do anything for them, they might die.

But I knew that this time, I couldn't jump in and save Casandra again. I had to let her figure this out on her own—as painful as that would be to watch.

Only a few days before being evicted from her current apartment, Casandra showed up to work with some good news. One of the families who had watched her oldest daughter the summer before had some connections at the local women's and children's shelter and had moved her name to the top of the list. The top! She would be the next one in when a bed opened up.

But moving into the shelter would mean that Casandra couldn't work at Better Life Bags anymore. The women's shelter had a two-year program they walked their residents through, and the daily bus ride to the Better Life Bags workshop would be too far of a commute. We were all sad thinking about our friend and sister not being with us every day. But if Casandra committed to this two-year program, she would graduate with an interest-free loan for a house of her own. The decision was a no-brainer.

I remember everyone gathering around her on her last day of work. Tears ran down my cheeks that no one could see because we all had our heads bowed as we prayed for this next chapter in her life. This felt like a failure. This leaving felt as though we had failed her. I wanted her income from Better Life Bags to be enough that she could afford her own home. Instead, she was moving into a shelter—the complete opposite. This felt like a huge step backward.

As Casandra walked down the sidewalk with her boys, leaving our workshop for the last time, I snapped a picture on my phone and felt God telling me that her story wasn't over. This wan't the end for her.

"I know, God," I whispered back, "I just wanted to be there to see the change."

And then I admitted what had been hiding in the dark shadows of my heart ever since I met Casandra. "I wanted to be the one credited for her miraculous turnaround, God. I wanted this to be the story to prove to everyone that Better

Life Bags does make lives better." We had been interviewed by handfuls of news stations and for printed articles and even a documentary that showcased the good work Better Life Bags was doing in Casandra's life. What if the media caught wind of this failure? I didn't want to imagine the embarrassing follow-up stories.

A few weeks after I watched Casandra walk away from the workshop, a message popped into my inbox from her. It was a note that changed my perspective: "Better Life Bags was life-changing for me," she wrote. "It was my first job ever and it felt like family. I loved cutting the purses out for the orders and everything about my job. I love and still appreciate you a lot for giving me a chance." Her message continued on to tell me that she had just been hired at a local nonprofit that focused on hiring women out of shelters to make winter coats that transform into sleeping bags for the homeless. Her years of cutting fabric at Better Life Bags had uniquely qualified her for a position at this company, which was much better equipped to help women who were clawing their way out of the poverty hole. She was even being considered for the program that would allow her to own her own home in two years. This is the Cinderella story I wanted for her all along. Maybe we did give her a better life after all. Not with a full TV-worthy transformation but in small significant ways that she would carry with her on the inside. Maybe we gave her the confidence and the life skills needed to land that next job. Maybe we helped her see that she was worthwhile and able to provide for her kids. Maybe we were her first step, not her finish line. We did not fail her.

When I think about it this way, is there such a thing as failure? Can we actually fail at something we set out to do? Or are the things that look like failures actually just small steps in a different direction? We may not get the credit for someone's life-change, but we can play a small part in their grand story. Our own failures are not steps backward. Every step counts. Ordinary shuffles forward are equally as important as the giant leaps—maybe even more significant. Little steps add up to a better life.

CHAPTER 11

Do Things That Are Unseen

You Don't Need to Share
Everything on the Internet

||||||||||||||||||||||||||||||||||||||||||||||||||||||||||||||||||||||

In college, I had a pretty unhealthy addiction to celebrity gossip magazines—the kind you are forced to read while you wait to check out at the grocery store. The loud fonts. The colorful pictures of perfectly flawless skin and new relationships and tragic breakups. It was all too much for me to turn away from. I was riveted by them. They jumped into my hands like metal to magnets. Of course, I would never subscribe to those magazines. I couldn't bear the shame of someone picking up my mail and uncovering my obsession with Jessica Simpson. Oh, the embarrassment! Plus, I was smarter with my finances than to spend actual, physical, hard-earned money on a flimsy, ink-stained collection of shiny pages. After all, I had taken Dave Ramsey's Financial Peace University in high school, and I was well trained in the art of managing my money.

But you bet I would find the longest grocery line—even allowing others to cut in front of me—so I could catch up on the goings-on in Hollywood. The Brad and Jennifer split? I couldn't believe it. They were so in love. Jessica Simpson and Nick Lachey and their adorable reality show Newlyweds: Nick and Jessica? Just take all my free time already. I was obsessed. I wanted to be them. I wanted to dress as she did, even going so far as making a necklace similar to the one she wore—since People told me the real one cost two thousand dollars. And Dave Ramsey haunted my bank account as much as Jessica haunted my desires. I wanted her high heels, her blond hair, her Daisy Duke legs, her husband, and her tan crocheted shawl that she casually threw around her shoulders in the most glamorous way. I wanted to say stupidly funny things that endeared me to other people. I wanted to feel the day-to-day exhilaration of being a celebrity. Known. Famous. I wanted people to praise the work I did and to want to see and hear more of it.

Around the same time as my celebrity gossip magazine obsession, I committed the summer of 2003 to being a counselor at Great Oaks Camp, a refuge for inner-city kids for one week out of every summer. I loved these kids. I wanted to bring them all home with me after their week was over instead of having them return to their homes. As each new group of campers rolled in on yellow buses, it became more apparent to me how different our lives were from each other. The stable, loving home I came from would be so foreign to their little eyes. I found myself suspended between this realistic world that my campers came from and the shiny, colorful images I envied on the pages of the gossip magazines.

I was in charge of arts and crafts, so I didn't have a regular cabin full of kids. I was, however, often used as the punishment station for bad behavior, especially for the boys' cabins. One time an entire cabin of boys misbehaved so badly that they were banned from the high ropes course and forced to spend an hour with me in the arts and crafts cabin. We sat in our screened-in, ten-foot by ten-foot wooden hut, surrounded by trees and bugs and humidity. I wondered how this was going to go. We made cross necklaces out of nails—the same kind of nails we envisioned Jesus being nailed to the cross with. And we talked about why this necklace was important and what the point of making crosses out of nails was. We talked about Jesus dying on a cross because we were full of sin and someone needed to pay the penalty for it. And we talked about how Jesus chose to do it on our behalf because he loved us so much.

At some point during the hour, it became quiet in the cabin as the boys continued to wrap twine around the nails. Then out of the blue, one boy turned to me—breaking the silence—and asked, "Is it true that there's someone out there that loves each one of us?"

Pull my heartstrings, will ya? Stick a dagger in it. This was a question one of them had been mulling over for the last ten minutes? Let me set the answer straight.

"Yes! It's absolutely true."

The boy sitting next to him stopped his jewelry-making to turn his eyes toward his friend. "I mean, God loves us."

And I assured the boys that each of the counselors here at camp loved them too, even if they had punished them with a trip to the arts and crafts cabin instead of the high ropes course.

I chose to sit with that group of boys at dinner that night. We rested our compartmentalized food trays on the round tables and sat on hard plastic seats still sticky from the morning's pancake syrup. Picking at his mac and cheese and hot dogs, the boy who had posed the question before turned his face toward me and asked again, "Do you guys really love us?"

It was such a small yet intimate privilege we counselors had that summer to tell kids for the first time that, yes, someone does actually love them. And I still wonder where those kids are today. I wonder whether those cross necklaces they made are cherished in jewelry boxes or hung from car mirrors as reminders that, yes, in fact, someone does love them.

At camp that summer, I developed a habit for coffee. I wore hemp necklaces, Goodwill T-shirts, and flip-flops. I didn't shower often. And I loved on those kids. I reluctantly called Child Protective Services when I had to. I visited them in their homes after the week of camp had ended. I continued Bible studies and kids' camps with them during the school year. And I started dating a fellow camp counselor who was equally as dirty and hemp-loving as I was. His lifestyle and look appealed to me too—musical, long hair, big eyes. Dating him made sense—we both loved inner-city kids and this camp counselor life. And while I wasn't particularly interested in a life forever with him, I desperately wanted my own version of Nick and Jessica. I mean, he would serenade me from outside my apartment window. It doesn't get more reality TV than that.

While talking to my fellow hemp-loving camp counselor about my obsession with gossip magazines, I found myself wondering about something. Maybe way up in the realm of heaven there were also celebrity gossip magazines. But instead of Nick and Jessica gracing the covers or getting the full-spread photoshoots, the magazines featured people like us. The ones getting dirty and walking into uncomfortable places to love inner-city kids. The ones who committed their lives to loving other people, even if media outlets and People magazine didn't cover the story. The ones doing things in secret just because they were the right things to do. Maybe we were on the magazine covers in heaven and angels found the longest lines at the grocery stores so they would have time to read our stories.

"Did you see what Rebecca did last week?"

"Can you believe it?"

"I can't wait to see what happens next!"

"Where do you think she gets her awesome T-shirts from?"

It seemed more appropriate to aspire to be heaven's celebrity than Hollywood's. As I tucked this truth away deep within my heart, the desire to lust after celebrity magazine life slowly faded away. I had a higher, longer-lasting goal to shoot for—the cover of Heavenly Today.

As Better Life Bags has grown, I've tasted a small part of the American celebrity life, willingly or not. Of course, People may never put my face on its cover, but some who have discovered Better Life Bags or my Instagram account have set me up on the celebrity pedestal of their minds.

I remember hearing about a young lady who couldn't make it to the annual warehouse sale Better Life Bags hosts in the heat of the summer most years. Her mom came instead and asked whether I would FaceTime with her daughter. Of course I would. I assumed the daughter had some important questions about which bag would be right for her daily life. But the moment I jumped on that call with her, she became a laughing, screaming, crying mess. I started laughing too—out of embarrassment and uncertainty about how to respond. And then the daughter told me that she felt as though she were meeting Justin Timberlake. Huh? Me and JT? Never would have seen that coming, I thought. The whole experience was rather unsettling. Especially because it felt kind of good. I was known. I was wanted. I was kinda famous. But now what?

In 2016 God dusted off the secret thoughts that had been hidden deep in my heart about the idea of those celebrity magazines in heaven. He blew hard, and the dust that flew up in the air caused me to sneeze back to reality.

Jennifer had been in her role as head seamstress at Better Life Bags for a few months when her mom got sick. She was dying. We knew it was coming, and we would ask Jennifer for updates regularly. Every time her phone rang, we held our breath, wondering whether today was the day. When her mom did pass away, all of us from Better Life Bags went to the funeral. A few of us carpooled there to make the initial entrance into a room full of strangers a bit less awkward. I sat inconspicuously on a hard pew in the back of the church, uncomfortable in my outfit and yet glad I had come to support Jennifer. But I could barely look past my overdue manicure and my snot-stained skirt. Why hadn't I noticed that before I left the house? More importantly, which tiny child of mine had felt that my skirt was an appropriate tissue for their runny nose? I was feeling "not enough" as I sat in the hard wooden pew.

But I soon realized this wasn't about me. This became plainly obvious as I opened the program and saw the face of a woman I'd never met. The one we were here to remember. The one I'd pictured in my mind a thousand times as I watched Jennifer walk through the last days with her mom. She looked nothing like I'd imagined. The face I saw in the program was smiling, and her hand was held up in a slight wave as if to say, "I see you. Thanks for coming and loving my family."

Her family. Oh, how they had loved this woman! Endless minutes were spent recounting memories and lessons learned from her. I hung on every word. She had taught piano lessons, she had passed on her gardening expertise to many, she had invested deeply in her children and taught them to love one another. She had supported her sister's family when they started a new life in America, selflessly choosing to share a room with her niece, as space was limited in their house. She had loved Jesus deeply and well. She had lived imperfectly—taking off her mask and showing others her real self—yet she had lived mightily as the woman God had created her to be. I felt tears coming to my eyes as I became acquainted with the life of this ordinary, spectacular woman.

And then I heard these words whispered deep within my soul: She is the famous one.

How could this be? She didn't have an Instagram account to feature all her good deeds. Only about fifty people knew her well enough to come and say goodbye. She hadn't documented her garden progress on her blog or advertised her piano lessons on Facebook. No one had lost their ever-loving minds when they'd FaceTimed with her.

She had simply lived her life with the people and the opportunities laid in front of her, with her head down and her praises unheard. Her passions were avenues of connecting with people, not trying to make a lasting mark on the world. Yet a mark she did leave. A deep one with permanent marker that not even hairspray can remove.

How many people out there are like Jennifer's mother? Ordinary people whom God is using to deeply impact the lives of others. Ordinary people who never get to share their stories with the world but so deeply deserve to. Ordinary people whose quiet lives lived out of the spotlight proclaim that God does use plain, ordinary people for his kingdom work.

I get called "famous" at least once a week. Sometimes in a joking manner from friends. Sometimes in an all-serious comment from an Instagram follower and fan of Better Life Bags. Yet I feel so ordinary. I can preach all day that God uses ordinary people to create a business that impacts a community, but somehow in the process of growing that company, I lost the "ordinary" badge.

This is true of almost every preacher, author, photographer, Instagrammer, and social entrepreneur. They stand in front of us and tell us they are ordinary and that God used them. But it's hard to believe them because they have grown past the boundary of what the world defines as ordinary. And so we need the people standing next to us to show us what living an ordinary, extraordinary life looks like. We need to see our neighbors, our family members, and our friends walk out what living extraordinarily in the most ordinary way looks like. And they need to see us doing the same. We need to believe for ourselves that God is using our everyday, small moments to make big differences in the lives of real people.

The larger my platform becomes, the less I'm able to convince others that it is the small, undocumented moments and the ordinary people God uses. But I promise you that everything starts small and seemingly insignificant, in a way that makes you wonder whether it's ever going to matter.

Here's the truth: If you're chasing fame, you may never reach the Instagram following you desire or write a New York Times bestselling book. You many never star on that endearing Newlywed-esque reality TV show. But why have we chosen these as the ultimate goals of influence and esteem? Maybe people like me—who speak and write and build businesses—are actually less effective in the kingdom now than when we first started. Maybe the classroom you teach in or the kids you tuck in at night or the small group you are a part of is your platform for loving people. And maybe that is more than enough.

I know you've heard this before, but have you really heard it, taken it the twelve inches from your head to the confines of your tender heart? God uses ordinary people to do extraordinary things! It's the ordinary people who do deep and lovely things for God in the quiet and the everyday who, I dare to say, are the true celebrities. These are the ones heaven writes about in its weekly celebrity gossip magazines distributed next to the pearly gates near Saint Peter's post.

These ordinary men and women love deeply and serve endlessly for no other reason or reward than that it is what they are called to do. These people get the Hall of Fame status in my book. These unsung heroes are the ones inheriting the rewards of heaven.

I want to sneak into the back of every memorial service I can find. I want to listen to the highlight reel of godly men and women—people without massive social media followings or bestselling books. I want to discover the people in the world who deserve true fame, who use their lives to do big kingdom work in super-small, unseen ways.

Jennifer's mom and her small yet big impact on her world so inspired me that at one point, I wanted to write a book highlighting the stories of women like her. Unknowns. Invisible souls. Women such as my friend, Ashley, who quietly and faithfully and mightily leaned on God while her five-year-old son battled a cancer with no cure. Another friend's husband, in addition to taking his own two girls to the yearly daddy-daughter dance, invites any of the girls' friends without fathers to join them. And doesn't post a single picture about it on social media.

Why does God ask some to share their stories with the entire world, while he has others live out their equally important stories quietly within the walls of their own homes? Why do we so often believe our words are not good enough unless they go viral? That the items we make are not worth anything unless many people buy them?

Who or what are we working for?

Here's what I believe: Public adoration is not the goal; obedience to our King is. Sometimes that obedience is played out on a stage with thousands of eyes watching us, but I think most obedience is done in secret.

What if we looked at the people in our lives and imagined what would be said about them at their funerals? What if we saw ourselves and others from the highlight reel of heaven and praised that? How would that change this life?

When people tell me I'm famous, I want to grab their cheeks in my hands and tell them, "No, you are! You, the woman doing dishes daily among the throng of toddlers. You, the woman faithfully serving meals to the homeless every month. You, the woman whose job it is to put a new bouquet of flowers on the church pulpit every week. I see you. You, the woman who checks out our groceries with a smile, no matter how bad your day was. You, the woman singlehandedly raising your children in this world. You, the woman who buys a house in the inner city and keeps her backyard open for all the kids to play in because God put a calling on your heart. You are the famous ones."

Let's take it one level deeper, okay? Let's give credit where credit is due. Those things we do in the secret and the quiet?

They weren't our idea to begin with, even if we woke up in the middle of the night with such a genius idea that we had to get up to write it down. Those ideas are from the One who designs and orchestrates everything to work together for good. If we take the simple steps of being obedient and faithful and keep showing up, we allow God room to move through us and make a deep impact on those around us. Those ideas are worth bragging about because they increase the fame of the One who sent us. And his celebrity should be the only concern on our hearts. Any fame or glory we receive is only a reflection of the stories and the things that God has done.

You know what really makes us famous? The stories and the things God has done in our lives. So let's share them with everyone. Let's boast of the fame of our King. Each one of us is famous—so, so famous—because of the stories God has brought to life in and through us.

What if the goal isn't to do big, famous things but to do great small things?

I think that when I get to heaven and look through the archives of the magazines that were once on display, I won't find a full-spread photoshoot of me with all the bags we've sold at Better Life Bags. But I will find a picture of myself with greasy hair, a braided hemp necklace, and a thrifted T-shirt, sitting in the arts and crafts cabin with all those boys, telling them that, yes, indeed, someone does love them.

CHAPTER 12

Have the Heart of a Turtle

Keep Your Eyes on Your Own Paper

||||||| |||||||||||||||||||||||||||||||||||||||||||||||||||||| ||||||||

One day I hopped on Instagram for some mindless scrolling in the midst of a toddler tantrum and messy kitchen. I had just discovered more poop smeared on my white walls, and I was done parenting. I couldn't do it anymore. I had to escape from my cluttered, smelly existence. After about three thumb swipes, my mind woke up to what I was seeing and the impact it was having on my heart in that moment. I realized I wanted to jump into all these curated images and live those perfect lives as my own. I wanted to leave my life behind and pick up these lovely Instagrammed lives instead.

Images of beautiful playrooms filled with handmade wooden toys displayed intricately on built-in shelves. Kitchen remodels complete with white subway tile, farmhouse sinks, and dreamy open shelving. Try-on sessions in dressing rooms, showcasing the latest trends, styles, and sales. Someone selling essential oils, trying to convince me that I too can make a six-figure income selling the same tiny bottles.

Through the wonder of Instagram, I was able to peek inside the lives of so many different women: stay-at-home moms, work-at-home moms, creative moms, empty nesters, full-time career women. It was all so inspiring—the captivating images and the imaginative videos. Life was presented as beautiful and tidy and accessible in those square images, even more so when I looked up from my phone to the mess of real life that was crawling toward me. If I imitated these women well enough, I figured I could have their lives instead of mine. Their example of what it looks like to live like them was right there in front of me.

I wanted to do it all. Everything I saw. I was ready to quit everything I was doing and start doing whatever they were doing. I wanted to be the DIY home blogger, the fashion blogger, the stay-at-home mom with all the creative ideas, the multilevel marketing maven, the home organizer, and the gourmet freezer-meal cook. It all seemed so possible. They made it look so easy.

Maybe when you look at all those Instagram images, you have the exact opposite reaction. Everything seems impossible. You know you'll never be a home blogger or a mom who cooks organic dinners from scratch every night. You'll never have a perfectly organized, painstakingly labeled pantry. And your closet will never look as minimal and put-together as those images on the screen. Scrolling your Instagram feed gets you down.

It's depressing either way.

Let's shift the perspective a bit, shall we? The reality is that we can't have anyone else's life. So look around and see your life in all its beautiful messiness and colorful chaos.

This is your path. This is your life. This is good news. None of that other stuff is for you! You don't have to cook extravagant dinners every night. Your closet doesn't have to consist of ten coordinating pieces that you wear until they fall apart. Your kids don't have to eat organic or learn watercolor. Maybe none of this works for your family. And maybe none of it works for you.

We have to realize that we are simply observers of other people's races. We are watching and seeing the progress others are making in their lanes, but we don't have to run with them. We have our own race to run—or walk—in our own lane and on our own path.

My lane has been paved for me and only me. White lines have been drawn for me specifically, and I am to stay within them, not as a punishment but as a guide so I can achieve and fulfill the good things God has planned for me. His good things lie within the white lines of my lane. They are not hidden from me, and they don't require a treasure hunt to find them.

I simply need to find my lane, stay in it, and try not to be distracted by everyone else running their own beautiful races in their own beautiful lanes.

Finding and staying in my lane with Better Life Bags has been a long process—and is something I still struggle with. I already mentioned how I originally started off in the wrong lane—the world of crafty DIY bloggers who wanted to make my bags instead of buy them. I quickly realized this and found the first exit. I wanted to get back on the highway and keep going. But I didn't know how. I thought I needed to find someone to lead me. To be the pacesetter. To tell me how to run and how far to run and how fast to run.

As I looked around for businesses that resembled mine,

I couldn't find many. Not many companies had a mission to hire women in America with barriers to employment, pay them well, and teach them to make custom leather and fabric handbags.

The handbag lane was out there, but I didn't fit in there. There were the high-end designer bags—Gucci, Coach, and Michael Kors. Their customers were not my customers. Their marketing strategies wouldn't work for us. Their pricing structures weren't the example we wanted to follow. We wanted to keep our margins slim to bring a product to market that wasn't inflated in cost.

We weren't like other ethical businesses either. We didn't face the same challenges or produce the same products. We were manufacturing in and hiring women from America—nothing was made overseas—this meant much higher wages. I couldn't jump into their lane and start running.

Eventually, I realized I needed to stop looking around for a lane to fit into and start traveling in the lane I was meant to be in all along. I looked at our unique business and started to walk on the path that had been specifically laid out for us. I didn't need to change lanes or find a new highway. I needed to look down and realize that my own lane where my own two feet had landed was the perfect one for me.

I also realized that I was the only one who could run Better Life Bags the way God wanted it to be run. I needed to step confidently into that role, knowing he would give me wisdom and creativity and fresh ideas. I needed to look at the poop my five-year-old had smeared on the walls of my home and realize that I am the perfect mother for these four children. I could wipe that poop off with a Clorox wipe and remind myself that these four precious lives have been given to me and that they are good.

I think it's less about finding the group you fit into and more about discovering and becoming the unique person God made you to be. Maybe these questions will help you discover your lane.

- What do you enjoy?
- What gifts and talents have you been given?
- What inspires you?
- What motivates you?
- What sends you into a spiral of depression and anxiety?
- What works for you?
- Which disciplines come easy, and which ones take practice?
- What lessons have you learned?
- What circumstances have you found yourself in?
- Where do you live?
- Who lives around you?

What can you do with all these puzzle pieces that make up the larger picture of who you are?

Don't worry about someone else's puzzle pieces or answers to those questions. They are for that person alone. Her life is different from yours. She has four kids. You have two. She loves reading. You prefer painting. She works full-time. You stay home. Her kids are grown up. You are in the throes of toddlerhood. Your lanes cannot and will not be the same. Yes, you can look to her as a running mate. You and she can inspire each other to keep running. You can set the pace for each other, but you cannot veer off into her lane. It's not yours. Her lane is for her. Your lane is for you. What works for her will not work for you.

You would think staying between two white lines would be one of the easier parts of driving. And a lot of the time it is, but there are going to be a lot of outside circumstances that try to push you out of your lane—temptations such as get-rich-quick schemes and grass-is-greener situations. Your lane may feel hard and unfair and dirty and crowded. And you may find yourself wanting to get out of it as fast as you can.

Have you ever been driving on a highway and suddenly found yourself in a construction zone where the normal white lines have been erased and the regular lanes have been replaced with temporary ones that are much narrower than usual? It's hard to focus on anything except staying in your tight little lane, isn't it?

You have to fight for your lane.

Your fingers grip the steering wheel a little tighter. Your mind blocks out any additional noise from kids in the backseat who are fighting over the McDonald's toy. Your eyes squint and zone in on those two painted white lines.

And then, instead of things getting better, a semitruck comes up on one side of you. You feel small compared with its giant, towering trailer. You hold your breath, hoping to suck and tuck the sides of your minivan in at the same time. You can feel the air trying to pull you closer to the semi's lane. You have to fight to stay in your lane—where you belong.

Finally, the construction zone is over, the lanes widen, and you settle back into a comfortable stance and pace. You exhale with relief.

You did it.

You stayed in your lane. You didn't succumb to the pressure to slow down or speed up. You didn't allow anyone to convince you to come into their lane or quit driving. The road felt like a tight squeeze, but you didn't give up. You stayed the course through all the construction and came out the other side unharmed—and maybe with a renewed sense of accomplishment.

In addition to finding your own lane and staying within your two white lines, no matter the pressure you feel to become like someone else, your next task is to find the pace that works for you. You don't have to run. You can walk. You can be slower than one girl. And you can be faster than someone else. Both are okay. And you can run with people. Or you can run alone.

I'll never forget the feeling I had as I was scrolling Instagram one day and came across a devotional book that had been written by creatives and for creatives. I recognized name after name in the collaborator list. These were my online coworkers. I'd held real conversations with them or met them personally. We had shared business struggles and successes over coffee at conferences. We had emailed deep and personal messages to each other.

My heart sunk as I realized I had been left out. I loved to write too. I was a creative too. I ran an online business too. I had a large platform of fans and customers and followers too. The organizers of the book knew me. I wondered why I hadn't been asked to contribute.

I felt like the turtle in the story of the tortoise and the hare. Everyone was passing me by—and fast. I was left in their dust—choking on it, actually—and trying to see through it enough to figure out what my next step would be.

It almost took me out of my race. I wanted to quit. I wanted to sit at the head table of my own pity party and cry. I wanted to lie down on the side of my figurative road and throw a temper tantrum—or take a nap.

And then after I was sad, I felt mad. I wanted to start running harder than everyone else. I had obviously been forgotten, so I wanted to get out ahead of everyone so I would be noticed. I wanted to beat everyone else and elbow anyone who tried to get ahead of me.

But I knew none of this would make me feel better. Feeling left out, looked over, and forgotten is terrible. To have others not acknowledge and recognize the things you are working so hard at really stings. It makes me wonder whether anything I'm doing is worthwhile. But we aren't living our lives for the sake of other people. Their opinions of us or our work or our family cannot determine our next steps. We cannot change what we are doing to please those around us if what we are doing is exactly what we know we're supposed to do. And as hard as it is to believe, there isn't enough time in the day to worry about who likes or doesn't like you. You gotta keep your head down.

I thought more about the turtle. He's confident in who he is. He takes sure and steady steps. He mutters under his breath to himself, "Just keep walking, just keep walking." He doesn't care where everyone else is in the race. He doesn't check the race standings—or his social media numbers—every hour. He's not mad if he's been left behind. He simply wants to finish his race at his own pace. He doesn't put on fuzzy ears and pretend to be a hare. He doesn't even try to get those four short legs to run. He doesn't build himself a go-kart or skateboard that might get him to the finish line faster. He just walks at his own steady pace.

I want to emulate him. His pace seems peaceful. His steps seem sure. His way seems obvious. His rhythm seems doable.

What if I had the heart of a turtle? What if after discovering my path and my purpose, I stayed surefooted and steady in my pace? What if I didn't impulsively rush to refinish my kitchen because I saw a sale on cabinets but instead saved and budgeted for that renovation on my kitchen and was okay with it taking longer to complete because it meant a peaceful heart? What if I were okay with Better Life Bags remaining a small company while my competitors reached Fortune 500 lists and were awarded Entrepreneur of the Year awards? What if I stopped comparing our social media numbers to those of other companies' and instead saw each follower as a person, being grateful that they were there instead of greedy for more?

||||||||||||||||||||||||||||||||||||||||||||||||||||||||||||||||||||

This bent toward comparison starts so young. Think back to early elementary school and those terrible timed math tests. My teacher would walk slowly around the room, placing a paper full of multiplication problems facedown on each desk and tapping her finger twice on the overturned paper before moving to the next desk in the row. We would all sit silently as we followed her slow stroll up and down the classroom rows. Finally, everyone would have their paper, and my teacher would stand at the front of the room with a timer. She would set it for five minutes, and before pressing the start button, she would count down, "Ready, set, go!" and a whoosh would blow throughout the classroom as we all flipped our tests over and started down the line of math facts.

Everything would feel good for a minute. But then Suzie would finish and loudly flip her paper back over and slam her pencil on her desk—signaling to everyone that she had finished first. My heart would beat faster.

I can't be last, I'd think. *Hurry—go faster.*

Then Tommy and David and Mackenzie would flip their papers and slam their pencils. I would look around the room to see who else was still frantically trying to figure out the answer to twelve times nine.

"Eyes on your own paper," my teacher would shout, jolting me from my comparison game and back to my own test. What I never seemed to understand was that this wasn't a race to finish first. I wasn't competing against Suzie or Tommy or David. I was racing against myself—in my own race—to see whether I could finish all the math facts by myself.

||||||||||||||||||||||||||||||||||||||||||||||||||||||||||||||||||||||||

I think I've become okay with not winning because winning has never been the goal. Just like that math test, life is not about winning—it's about finishing. Finishing well is what we should all aim for. I've been given an incredible company. What will I do with it? Will I steward it well and focus on the women we hire and the products we offer and make? Or will I be distant from them, my eyes darting back and forth from company to company, trying to figure out how to beat them and do everything better or faster than they can? Will I love on the customers that have come our way? Will I listen to them, take their feedback, and create products I know they will love? Will I create a company we all are proud of—one that is honest and slow and steady and meaningful? What would it look like to finish well with Better Life Bags?

I've been given a family with four wild little kids. Will I zone out and try to escape from the chaos as often as I can? Will I busy myself with organizing and cleaning instead of reading to them and crowding around a board game? Will I look at families with two kids and wish my life were a little less crazy? Will I take the time to lie in their beds at night and ask them how their days were? Or will I rush bedtime so that the day can finally be over? What would it look like to finish well in the parenting journey? What would I need to do to sit in a quiet home after all the kids have grown and not regret one moment?

Let's put off the idea that we need to finish first. Let's quit looking at the people running on either side of us and get our eyes back on our lanes. Let's decide that we will walk our own journeys with strength, confidence, and humility. Let's cheer others on when we see them pass us. Let's encourage those stumbling behind. Let's keep our eyes on our own papers. Let's put on our turtle shells and enjoy the walk.

CHAPTER 13

Lean In to Hard Times

When God Tells You That
You're a Palm Tree

||||||||||||||||||||||||||||||||||||||||||||||||||||||||||||||||||||||

Want to know a little secret? Can I pull back the curtain a little more?

Things haven't always been easy. There have been a lot of hard times as I've built this better life.

We have had incredible growth in Better Life Bags over the years—overwhelming growth sometimes. Months have often beaten the month's sales from the year before. Our product line has expanded. We started with one diaper bag—the Emily—and now have tote bags, messenger bags, laptop bags, wallets, nesting pouches, and backpacks. Each bag is named after someone in the Better Life Bag family—a seamstress, a customer, or even after the bags themselves. When a customer requested a miniature version of the Linda bag, we named it Melinda (mini Linda). Sometimes this growth felt too easy. I knew God's hand had to be on this business because it seemed as though everything I touched turned to gold. It was fun. Making money is always fun.

But losing money is not fun. So when we eventually experienced periods of slow growth—after becoming used to such extravagant growth—it didn't feel good.

I have this not-so-fancy chart hanging on my bulletin board at work. It tracks monthly sales from month to month and year to year. I use a mechanical pencil and white computer paper to draw wonky lines between years and months. At the end of each month, I get so excited to look at the month's sales and write it up there, in line with each year previous. It's a quick pulse check to see how we're doing.

One month the numbers were less than the year before. By a lot.

Hmmmmmm, I thought. I don't really like that. Must have been a fluke.

Except it kept happening. Month after month.

One night I was up particularly late and feeling incredibly anxious. We were going on several months of sales that were much lower than our operating budget. Forget meeting the previous year's month of sales. We just needed to make enough to pay rent and make payroll—and I wasn't sure that was going to happen.

It doesn't take a business major to realize that if you are bringing in less than you are spending, the numbers aren't going to add up. It's only a matter of time until the decline is more than the business can handle, and something will break under the weight of the pressure.

It's the ugliest truth in the world because it applies to so many things that are just plain hard and seemingly unfair. If you eat more calories than you burn, you'll gain weight. If you spend more than you make, you'll go into debt. If the payroll is higher than the sales coming in, someone is going to have to be let go.

Should it be me first? Should I cut my own salary to save the livelihoods of my seamstresses?

The problem was that this was our livelihood too. Our family relied solely on the salary I made from Better Life Bags. There was no alternative income. This was not our second income. Or our fun money. This was it. This was what put food on our table and paid our bills. All our eggs were in this basket—or bag, if you will.

But maybe a good leader cuts her salary before cutting anyone else's.

I contemplated the idea that we might have to move into my parents' basement—if they let us. I imagined where our pictures would hang and which pieces of furniture we would keep, which pieces we would sell, and which pieces we would store. I took inventory of everything in our home and categorized each item as keep, sell, or store.

I could not sleep.

I tried taking my mind off the business by playing 2048 on my phone. It was a game I had become increasingly addicted to—each time trying to get a higher and higher number by mashing similar numbers together. Twos became fours. Fours became eights. Eights became sixteens. Sixteens became thirty-twos. And on and on until you reached the tile 2048. But every time you smashed number tiles together, another one appeared in a random spot on the board. If you didn't play your swipes correctly—right, left, up, or down—you'd make a devastating move, and the game board would quickly fill up without one match to be seen.

Game over.

It felt a lot like my life right then. So many choices and decisions about which way to swipe. How was I going to get us over this horrific string of low sales? Why the sudden drop in sales?

It felt as if someone might be playing a mean trick on us and blocking our website from showing up on the internet. Just to be sure, I checked. I pulled open my phone and typed in our website address. There it was. Bright and colorful and full of products I was proud of. So why were sales so low?

I tried sleeping, but my mind was racing. Tossing and turning and trying to will yourself to sleep is one of the worst feelings in the world. My eyelids started shaking from trying to stay shut. The bedsheets became hot and tangled from all the twisting and restlessness. I finally got out of bed.

My cell phone told me it was 1:18 a.m. I walked downstairs, opened my laptop, and started writing. The words were not pretty, and after twenty minutes I was sure I wouldn't be able to use any of them in my book. But I wrote. Mostly to God. Mostly about how I felt like a failure and a fraud. How ironic was it that I was writing this book loosely based on how Better Life Bags had grown from a hobby to a business, and now it all seemed to be crumbling faster than my fingers could type?

I pictured having to email my agent and publisher to explain that the book was about to take a sharp left turn and become a story about how embarrassing it is to fail in front of thousands of people. I envisioned the last chapter being a massive plot twist announcing the closing of Better Life Bags.

I asked God where he was in all this. I find this is one of the most common questions I stumble into asking—no matter what challenges I'm currently going through. "God, where are you right now?" Usually I'm so mad that he doesn't seem to care about my problems and my life that I ask it in an angry and accusatory way. But every single time, I've heard him answer me. It never fails.

That night he said, "Calm down. Be still. Wait. Sit quietly in this darkness. Don't be anxious. Steady your heart. Trust me."

Trust him? It had been months of repeating to myself that God was in control of sales. That there was a purpose in the slowness. That he would provide. Enough was enough! It was time to take things into my own hands. He clearly didn't see us and obviously hadn't logged into our bank account in a while. Otherwise, he would be moving fast. Instead, his slowness was painful. And I felt panicked—as though I needed to act now.

I contemplated hiring one of those planes with the banners trailing behind to advertise www.betterlifebags.com. I wondered how much that would cost. Maybe I could post something on my Facebook page reminding all my family and friends that Better Life Bags could sure use some love. We were still here, waiting for orders. Perhaps I could somehow force the most loyal Better Life Bags customers to share our website with ten of their friends who had not heard about us.

Then I spiraled further into anxious despair. Tears started falling—hot, wet ones. Here I was writing a book about trusting that God has good plans for our lives that we don't have to chase anxiously after. About being obedient to keep my hands off and let God pave the path. About digging my roots deep into the soil I found myself in—even when it wasn't where I wanted to be. Seeing a business sprout out of that soil from a very small seed. Asking God for the mission and the purpose behind what I was doing. Crossing boundaries and lines that felt uncomfortable and reaching my hand across cultural divides anyway. Letting my dreams simmer a bit before killing them with my fear, then creating boundaries around how much and when I would hustle after them. Not doing this thing alone and realizing how much I needed the specific team God was building for me. Learning to do things in secret and without a lot of fanfare or awards while having the heart of a turtle, keeping my head down and walking my own walk. Every chapter was filled with examples of how being faithful and obedient and avoiding the hustle had built this better life that was indeed better than anything I could have constructed on my own. But maybe I'd been terribly wrong this entire time, and it was finally catching up to me.

I called myself a fraud—right there in black and white on my computer screen. I spelled it out: F-R-A-U-D. Sometimes it helps to get all the feelings out in order to move on to the truth.

The truth came easier now that my emotions were all out there. I stopped emotional typing and thought quietly for a while. I tried to remind myself of the truth. Even if this was the end, God was still good. If my race with Better Life Bags was over before I felt ready, I would finish well—sales or no sales. God works *all* things together for the good of those who love him. All things. Romans 8:28 doesn't say he works all *good* things together for good. It says he works *all* things together for good. All things. Even the seemingly embarrassing end to my writing career and my nine-year-old business on the same night. It was for my good. How could I not want it?

If this was the end, he would come through with peace and closure and a next step. And if this wasn't the end, he would come through with orders and customers and another day in business.

I closed my laptop, not because I was done writing but because it was about to die and I couldn't find my charger in the darkness of night. I lay back down in my bed and turned on some children's lullaby piano music, anything to make it through this night. Right before my brain finally surrendered to slumber, I heard it. That cha-ching sound effect on my phone.

Some wonderful soul, up late as well, had made a purchase on our website! And I thanked God while a soft, sleepy smile spread across my face. He did see. I don't know what he had been waiting for—I had been begging to hear that noise all day. But something happened that night. Besides the sale of a Linda bag, my soul was encouraged. My anthem of waiting—of stillness, of quiet faithfulness—had been reinforced. He was in control and needed me to stand down. I needed to keep my hands off but my heart engaged with him. Good things do come to those who wait.

The very next day, after months of meager sales, we recorded one of our best days of the year. I can't say something magical had happened the night before, except that I had been desperate and anxious, and instead of hustling harder, I had chosen to pray. I had begged God to move. I had reminded myself that even if this was the end, he was still good. He would still provide. I would not need to be embarrassed by failure, because he held the future.

While I was up so late that night, the story of Job kept coming to my mind. Now, I don't pretend to compare our shortage of sales to the extreme amount of loss Job experienced with his livestock, servants, and seven sons and three daughters all dying because of invaders or natural catastrophes. And then a terrible skin disease on top of it all. It's not the same loss, but I did want to emulate Job in my response to my challenges.

Job was sad, yes—deeply. He tore his clothing and didn't speak for an entire week. But he also desperately wanted God to be glorified. The cool thing about this story is that we get a peek behind the curtain—a look behind the scenes—into heaven. Before tormenting Job, Satan basically tells God that Job is "blameless" and "upright"—always careful to avoid doing evil—only because God has blessed him abundantly. Job was a wealthy man with a large family and extensive flocks.

This was me. I pinch myself daily at the dream job I have and how seemingly easy everything has fallen into place. Despite two early miscarriages, we've never struggled to have children or walked the road of infertility. We have a very comfortable salary—we are able to save money in a retirement account and an investment account—and my husband is able to be home with us more days that not. We can travel and have flexibility with our schedule—one of the biggest reasons people start working for themselves.

We have it made. God has blessed us immensely.

I imagined Satan up there conversing with God about me, saying, "She only worships you and gives you credit for this business of hers because you have been generous to her. You've spoiled her. Let me drastically reduce sales for her business and simultaneously make her second-guess this book she's writing, and I'll show you what she's really made of, God. She will surely turn and curse you—just watch."

I did not want the enemy to win. I was willing and determined to stand through whatever flames and testing Satan was going to throw at me. I would bend—and be honest about how horrible this all felt—but I would not break. I would not blame God or call anything a mistake.

I contemplated googling what to do in a situation where God has given you a thriving business for nine years, but suddenly it's dying. But I knew what I'd find in the pages of that search: boost your Facebook ads, hire a public relations firm, raise prices, create a new product line, hustle harder. Or, possibly, I'd find the answer that would seemingly relieve all the pressure and problems—just quit.

Thankfully, my friends were not quite as negative as Job's friends. Even his wife told him to curse God and give up and die. Now, the poor sweet woman was also deeply mourning the loss of her ten children, so we shall extend some grace to her. But I'm so grateful that even while I was trying to figure out what I had done wrong to directly result in a decrease in sales, none of the people I reached out to suggested this as an option. No one asked me what sin I had committed to cause this to happen. Everyone rallied around me, reaffirming the promises of God to provide and come through.

Our management team at Better Life Bags spent part of our Monday morning meeting praying and asking God to continue to provide for everyone in whatever way he saw appropriate. After I publicly shared the raw truth that sales were low and I was scared, some of my Instagram followers immediately messaged me with their prayers and reminders that it didn't seem like a coincidence to them that some spiritual warfare might begin just as I started to write a book about trusting God above all else.

Even my accountant, whom I had reached out to via an SOS email that night I was up worried and praying, reminded me that we were not dead. He would for sure tell me if we were. And he spent a generous amount of time brainstorming with me about some practical ways to make it through tight times.

It's always fun to bring people inside when things are going well, to show off the fun and the shiny and the perfect. The baby showers are a thousand times more fun than the quiet prayer circles called in the late hours of the night to beg God to stop the bleeding of a miscarriage. But those people kneeling next to you with their hands on your emptying belly? They are the ones you remember. No one can recall who bought the bouncy seat off your registry, but we can recall the names of people who sat through the muck with us in the hardest times of our lives. These are the people we allow to view the valleys so that they can praise God with us when he finally brings us up and out. These are the people we lean on as we are leaning in to the hard times.

While it had been the first, this would not be the last time I would stand at the edge of a cliff with the business and wonder how we were going to make it one more week. Our bank account would reach frighteningly low numbers. A surprise bill would show up in the mail. Our sales would take another dip. Every time, I had a panicky feeling as if this might be the end. And maybe someday it will be—maybe someday God will tell me I've run the race and it's time to sit down. But that day is not today. So I keep walking.

I'm sure all of us reach points in our lives where we feel as though it's the end. Maybe your marriage is barely hanging on, or your children are making choices you don't agree with. Maybe they are downsizing at work, or your house is about to go into foreclosure. These are super hard realities, some that I've walked through personally. And when we are in them, it seems as though God is being quiet, or even that he doesn't care. It's a logical conclusion. But it's a lie. He is working all things together for good, and there is great purpose in the struggle. We may not see it yet, but someday we will. We have to lean in to the hard times instead of running from them. We have to lean in so we can be in the best position to listen.

I should not have been surprised to encounter this trial. God had told me it would come. A few years ago, I was practicing a type of prayer called "listening prayer." It involves asking God questions and listening for an answer. I was new to this type of prayer and wrote down the first thing that came to my mind after asking God a question. Unless it sounded anti-biblical, I assumed it was a message from him.

During one of these prayer times, I asked God how he viewed me, what he saw when he looked at me. Immediately a palm tree came to my mind. It seemed crazy at first until I thought more about palm trees. They are made to withstand lots of wind. While most trees would snap under the intense pressure of hurricane winds, palm trees simply bend. They lean in.

I pressed God further and asked, "What does this mean?"

"I've created you to withstand hard times," I heard him whisper to my soul. "You will experience devastating seasons in your marriage, but you will not crack. Your mothering journey will not be an easy one, but I have built you to last. You will bend as the wind and waves of life blow hard against you, but you, my sweet child, will not break."

He has built me to lean.

CHAPTER 14

Cherish Today

Stop Wishing for the Next Season
of Life and Start Living Today's

||||||||||||||||||||||||||||||||||||||||||||||||||||||||||||||||||||||||||||

Tell me if this sounds familiar.

You're seventeen years old, a senior in high school, and all anyone can ask you about is where you're going to go to college and what you're going to major in. You finally choose a college and a major, pack up all your belongings, and move into the dorms.

On the first day of class, you meet a cute guy, and after a few dates, the two of you decide to make it official. Months later everyone starts whispering and wondering and asking when the two of you are going to get engaged. He finally pops the question, and you, of course, scream yes and change your Facebook status to "engaged" and post a picture of your new diamond. After everyone's exclamations of congratulations, they immediately want to know when the wedding will be.

Your honeymoon isn't even over yet when family members start dropping hints about having kids. And while you are still pregnant with your first child, people start asking how many more kids you hope to have.

What's next? What's next? What's next?

It's never-ending and dizzying to think about. Sometimes, everything in life feels as though it's focused on the "what's next" mentality. If you're not careful, your life can start to resemble a rat race. As soon as you've reached the end of one tiny maze, the "wall" opens, and you realize there is an entirely new race to run. It's exhausting. We reach one stage of life—earn a degree, get married, or have a baby—then the finish line moves, and we need to keep running. There's no time to each the cheese. Living life this way means there is no time to sit and enjoy the season of life you're in, because your eyes are always focused on what's to come.

There is a better way. There is a way to live this life and fully enjoy the moment. We can wake up to how fragile and fleeting this life is in comparison to eternity and make our days memorable and our relationships important. We can sit in the moment—the today—look around, and be grateful for what we have without wishing for the next season of life.

As Better Life Bags was growing, podcasts had begun popping up left and right. In these early days of podcasts, I was asked to be a guest on quite a few. And no matter who was interviewing me, one thing never failed. After hearing the story of my hobby getting bigger, the hiring of Nadia, the leather being added to the bags, the hiring of more women, and my realization that this was an actual business, one of the last questions of the podcast would always be: "So, what's next for Better Life Bags?"

I realize this was a genuinely curious question and perhaps fair to ask a person who runs a business that needs to keep growing and changing in order to thrive. But, honestly, I never quite knew the answer to that question. And I wondered why the answer mattered so much. Why did everyone want to know? It seemed to minimize all the stories I had just shared. The "what's next?" always sounded as though I hadn't done enough already. As if starting a business, navigating taxes, and hiring women from our under-resourced neighborhood wasn't enough. That there had to be something more. Another goal to reach. Another race to run. Another definition of success.

Maybe that's the problem. Everyone's definition of success skews the conversation. I had felt very successful in transitioning a hobby into a business and was so proud to have fifteen skilled women from Hamtramck working at Better Life Bags. Success to me would be maintaining that. Success to someone else might be making $1 million of product per quarter. Success to another might be selling the business for a profit and starting something new. But what if my business never grew beyond these fifteen women in Hamtramck? Would that mean I had failed? I didn't know the answer to that. So I'd muddle my way through the interview, telling them something I thought they would want to hear.

"We're hiring another woman!" But as it turns out, we weren't able to. In fact, over the next year, we lost five employees. Some moved, one took another job, some decided to take care of sick relatives and no longer had time to sew, and one seamstress went to school to become a medical assistant.

"We're coming out with a few new bag styles this year!" We did. We continue to tweak our current designs and add new ones as the years go on, and we get feedback from our customers on bags they wish we would make.

"I'm hoping to start designing and printing our own fabric by the end of 2018!" While we have a few prints exclusive to our company, we didn't quite meet this goal. It ended up being a huge financial investment that I didn't want to take on. A digital printer was hundreds of thousands of dollars and brought with it challenges of its own. We would need to hire someone to run the machine, fix it if it broke, and make sure the ink was performing at the highest quality.

"There are some conversations happening about starting a new Better Life Bags location in another city!" You know this story. We never did.

One day I got tired of it. I got tired of feeding into the lie that we were not okay right where we were. That our fifteen-woman, six-figure business was somehow mediocre compared with others around us. And my answers to those frequently asked questions changed.

"You know," I'd quietly start out, "if we remain exactly the same size for the next twenty years, I'll consider that a success. Even if we get smaller but still invest well in the people God has put in our company, we will be winning. We don't have big plans to grow or lots of money invested in marketing campaigns. We are simply doing our best to follow God's leading and step into the opportunities he sends our way—your podcast being one of them!"

The podcaster would wholeheartedly agree, and I hoped my message of being okay where you are would reach the heart of someone listening. Growth does not always equal success. Sometimes the best plan for your dreams—and even your business—might be to stay the same size you are now. Or—gasp!—even get smaller.

The Bible instructs us in 1 Thessalonians 4 to lead a quiet life—to mind our own business and work with our hands. This is extremely hard to do when today's world of social media is shouting at us that big is better than small and explosive growth is better than growing slowly.

I've learned along the way that it's not about the destination. It's not about the finish line or checking off the final task on the list. The real living happens in the journey of getting there. The lessons, hardships, challenges, and celebrations of today are the moments we are asked to enjoy—to be present for.

I went into my daughter's room the other night and leaned over her bed to kiss her goodnight. She put her hands up and grunted while scrunching up her face and turning it from me. It was clear that she didn't want a goodnight kiss from me. I stood back up and gently rebuked her. "No. We don't do this. We don't know when this might be the last night we will see each other. We have to take all the opportunities to say 'I love you' and give out hugs and kisses to people we love. It's not worth the risk to play these games."

Her face turned toward me as she realized for the first time that this life is temporary.

"You mean you're going to die tonight?" she asked with tears pooling in her eyes.

"We don't know, little love. We don't know when our last moments together will be, so we have to really live out the ones we know we have—the ones right now."

I lay down in her bed and held her until she fell asleep, inhaling the smell of her hair and watching her chest rise and fall with each breath. I counted the freckles on her cheek and noticed the way her eyelashes curl up when her eyes are closed. This was my moment with her—I was guaranteed this one but not the next. We are not guaranteed tomorrow. No one has modeled this more than my friend Ashley. We lived in the same apartment complex as her and her husband, Josh, when we lived in Savannah. Wanting to join our mission to invest in the people of Hamtramck, they moved up to Michigan a year after we did. She was there with Better Life Bags in the corners of my house since the beginning. Our kids would play together in Jonah's bedroom while Ashley and I finished packaging orders. She would answer as many customer emails as she could, becoming our first design helper.

Our lives were so connected here in Hamtramck. We often clung to each other as one of the only familiar-looking faces in the city. We ate chocolate-chip-cookie cake on her birthday, devouring it all in my tiny living room before Fat Tuesday was over and we would start our fast from sugar for the next forty days. She would make Starbucks runs to the closest location twenty minutes away and bring coffee back to enable us to work late into the evening together. And we would hit the McDonald's drive-through in town for dinner before heading back into the workshop to answer emails and to ship more orders.

One day Ashley and Josh sat Neil and me down on our couch and told us they were moving back to Georgia. Things weren't working out for them here, and they needed to go back. They were so far from family. The winters were so cold. The jobs for Josh were lacking. But mostly, they felt a pressing need from God to move home. We would soon find out why.

I was so sad. Sad to be losing my friend. Sad to be losing friends of my children. Sad to be losing a chapter of Better Life Bags.

A few months after Ashley and her family settled back in humid—but beautiful—Savannah, Georgia, I got an email from her with the subject line "Cancer."

Her John. Her five-year-old John had just been diagnosed with cancer. And not the good kind—as if any kind can be good. It became a matter of prolonging his life until a cure could be found—which was hopefully soon. The cure wasn't found in time, and we said goodbye to John in October 2018, one week before I gave birth to Gavin. Death and birth all within seven short days. It was a lot for me to process, and I imagined that Ashley was reeling.

As we've talked together in these recent months after losing John, remembering his life and visiting the places in Michigan that he loved, I've been reminded again that this life is temporary. Half of Ashley's heart now lives in heaven, while she continues to put one foot in front of the other here on earth. But she calls herself "one of the lucky ones." She wrote this in a Facebook post:

> When John was diagnosed in June 2016, something in me broke. It was a very good and necessary breaking. My ultimate worst fear had come true. My son was nowhere near perfect. He was so sick, and God used his disease to surely plant my hope elsewhere. My hope is not in my kids, their abilities, or their futures. The dreams that I used to dream for our kids and our family now seem so futile. This world and all its desires are passing away, and I'm so grateful for God—the dream crusher—who uses these hard life circumstances to train us. Those of us with sick kids just might be the lucky ones in light of eternity.
>
> Troubles really are light and momentary in this life. This is a short ride that we are on.... While we are grateful and take pictures along the way, we remember who God is, what He has done, and what He is capable of doing again. He is doing miracles every day that have nothing to do with neuroblastoma. Cancer is His useful tool. And while we wanted God to heal our son's body so much, we need Him to heal our sick hearts so much more. Have I ever said this? GOD IS GOOD.

I often think about those days in Hamtramck together and remember the crazy, the fun, the hard. The days before cancer. The days before heartbreak. The days when all we had to worry about was getting orders to the post office before customers started emailing and wondering when they would ship.

Those were the days. But did we know it at the time? Did we treasure those moments and try to spend every millisecond we could in them? Do we know that today—the day you are reading these words on this page—is the day we will long for in the future? Do we realize that these are the days? The ones happening right now.

Ashley gets it. She gets that this life is short, because she lived out that reality when she buried her seven-year-old son. And she considers herself lucky to have learned that lesson so vividly—one that she will never forget and one that has shaped the living of her days from then on.

These are our actual days that we will look back on in five or ten years and long for. The days of small beginnings when everything is scrappy and we are working in the margins of life to bring some dream to the surface. The days of wiping butts and wiping mouths and going through so many wipes we're sure we've killed an entire forest single-handedly.

Everything has a season. That Instagram celebrity you see selling millions of books and webinars like penny candy at the dollar store? Her moment won't last. Her following will eventually find someone else to obsess over. Even Miss America gets her crown for only one year. None of our moments will last. Our children will not remain small forever. The days of puzzle-making, crayon art, and popsicles on the front porch in the heat of summer are fading fast. We never know when our time will be up. So we should live every day as if it's our last. Not necessarily by going skydiving and climbing Mount

Everest, but by living well and small and deep—walking confidently on the path laid out before us, knowing it has been planned and prepared for us. And that it is good.

I'm especially grateful for my Better Life Bags journey and this path God has led me on. It feels strange to write this book now, when I'm still in the midst of running this company. I don't know how the story ends. I don't know when this chapter of my life will be over or where the business will go next or how long our season will last or how many lives we will impact—both locally and nationally, as people hear our story and are encouraged to start missional businesses of their own.

I don't know whether I'll sell the company someday or still be working there alongside my kids in thirty years. Maybe I'll never know the legacy we left behind as we kept our heads down on our own path and walked deliberately, one foot in front of the other.

Maybe that's why writing this book now—before the story is over—is when God wanted me to write it, so that we could all be reminded that the middle is the good stuff.

These are the actual days. The days for a quiet life. A deep life. A meaningful life. Look up and look around. This, right here, is our better life.

A Better Life Manifesto

This life is a good one. It's a gifted one and a fragile one. It's one full of sunny days spent lounging poolside and one with powerful thunderstorms best watched from porch chairs. Both are days equally well spent. Both are adding to the variation of life and seasons we adore.

This life is given to us. It's not ours to orchestrate or manipulate. We listen for the voice of our Creator and do what he says. We move when he says move. And we keep our hands off when he tells us to be still. He is orchestrating our days. He planned them for us before we ever took our first breath—both the easy days and the hard ones. Both are leading us to a beautiful life.

This life is ours to dig into. This place is where we stand. This neighborhood is our mission field. These people around us are our community. We don't wish for something different or run from where we've been planted. We will dig our roots in deep and bloom right where we are—no matter how hard the soil may feel. If flowers can push their way through cracks in the sidewalks, nothing is impossible.

This life starts small. It starts as a single thought. One act of love determines someone's next eighty years. The beginnings are the beautiful starts. We won't miss them or hurry through them. We will celebrate progress instead of waiting for perfection.

This life isn't only ours to live. It also belongs to those around us. We are here to tear down fences and build bridges of trust. We are here for a specific purpose.

We are here to love others in creative ways. We are here to make lives better and leave them changed. We will take a moment to make someone smile. We will stop whatever we are doing to wrestle in the grass with our kids. We will put people over projects.

This life is full of opportunity. We will nurture the dream in our hearts and see where it leads. We won't be afraid to make U-turns. We won't be embarrassed to fail. We will invite others to join us because we see the gifts they can bring to the table—gifts that make us whole.

This life has enough for us all. We will cheer instead of compete. We will keep our eyes on our race and run with integrity and grace. We will rally around other people's dreams and cheer them on. We will set up boundaries for the hustle and trust God for the growth. We will believe in this better way.

This life won't be easy. We will encounter storms and trials and pain. We will lean into them even though they hurt. We will ask God to hold us and comfort us, and he will. He will also remind us that we were made for this and that this is part of a life well lived. It will not break us.

This life is so short. It's a tiny blip on an ever-expanding timeline. It's one we could miss if we blink too long. We will not buy in to the "grass is always greener" lie. We will not wish the days away and long for what is next. We will see each ordinary moment as extraordinary. We will remind ourselves that these are the days.

This life is today. It won't become better when we reach our next goal. It's already spectacular because it's our own. We photograph the days in our mind and build a beautiful scrapbook. We write down the moments that make us laugh. And we mark the times when everything feels too hard. We ask God to show us he's there, and we notice the stickers he leaves for us, telling us we are special. We will stop striving for bigger and start seeing the small as sacred.

We will see this life for what it is. This life—right here—is our better life.

Acknowledgments

Ever since I started writing a book, this section has become the first place I flip to when I read other books. I love seeing all the people who played a part in helping a book-baby come to life. And then as I've written my own book, it's become even more important to have a place to write the names of those who have linked arms with me, watched my kids, brought over dinner, answered my questions, or texted encouragements.

Alicia Kasen—who saw something in me before I even saw it myself, who saw this book and its message as important before I even knew what it would be about.

Lisa Leonard—who texted me to tell me that the world would be better for having my book in it.

Jess Connolly—who early on told me that I would need to start speaking life to myself, and boy, were you right.

Hayley Morgan—for answering all my silly questions about how to save documents to compile a book.

Yanni and David Nevue—whose melodies carried me through writing each chapter.

My VIP Facebook group—who cheered me on and made me feel better when I would eat an entire box of Girl Scout Cookies while writing.

Lisa Jackson—whom this book would be nothing without. Thank you for being my "writing buddy."

Mom and Dad—who kept every early book I'd ever written and provided every opportunity for me to have the flexibility and financial freedom in life to even think about writing.

My brothers, Tyler and Kyle—who helped name Better Life Bags and designed the first logo and have always been my biggest fans.

Elise—who may not have birthed Better Life Bags, but you sure have been its beloved nanny and helped it grow up. Thank you is not enough.

Jennifer—the head seamstress I told Elise didn't exist. And then there you were. What a gift.

Nadia—my dear, dear friend. Thank you for being there for me and BLB. Thank you for sewing so many bags and always greeting me with a hug. You have changed my life.

All the seamstresses at BLB—the way you embrace and own the company as your own is a gift to me. I'm so grateful for you.

Matt—you never freaked out after reading my late-night SOS emails. You truly are the best accountant there is.

Kate—for being the first internet friend to post about BLB, causing a frenzy for blue-and-white herringbone Molly bags.

Rachael and Kacia—thank you for being so ahead in design trends to even think to ask for leather on your bags.

Natalie, Jessica, Melody, and Megan—that first initial mastermind group we created was everything I needed to keep going in those early days. I'm so grateful for those calls.

Joy Cho—You don't know me, but your simple little Pinterest pin changed everything.

Isabelle, Liz, and Le Detroit Macaron—besides being my

friends and dropping off "finish the book" care packages, thank you for making the most delicious macarons ever.

Ashley—you have been the truest example of how to live a better life. Thank you for sharing your words, your memories, and your time with me and BLB.

Emily—the best friend I've never met. Thanks for solving all the world's problems with me.

The DP moms—it's early, but I already feel so known.

To everyone that I forgot—it will haunt me for the rest of my life. Just consider everything you did to help me write this book as your good deeds done in secret. I hear there are rewards in heaven for those.

My kids—I can't wait to watch your little lives unfold as you walk your unique paths that God has designed for you. You can bet I'll be cheering you on the whole time.

Neil—you told me to keep writing even when I hated the words coming out. You believed in me—and Better Life Bags—and have sacrificed so much of you to invest in us. I'm so glad you answered that profile message and stuck around. I love you.

And God—thanks for the sticker.

better life BAGS

custom with a cause

Join us in our effort to provide meaningful work for women in Detroit and the world.

Visit www.betterlifebags.com to check out our product line and experience our interactive design software that lets you create and design a custom bag right before your eyes.

Every purchase directly employs a woman with barriers to traditional employment.

Rebecca